TWO TRUTHS AND A LIE THAT SET ME FREE

TWO TRUTHS AND A LIE THAT SET ME FREE

DENISE J SMITH

Queen Jungle Productions

Contents

1 Denial — 4

2 Jasmine and Bobby — 66

3 Nicole and Robyn — 83

4 Veronica and Gloria — 108

5 Erika — 139

6 Freedom — 163

Copyright © 2021 by Denise Smith

All rights reserved. No part of this book may be reproduced in any manner whatsoever without written permission except in the case of brief quotations embodied in critical articles and reviews.

First Printing, 2021

TWO TRUTHS AND A LIE THAT SET ME FREE

DENISE J SMITH

Thank you, Mother, for your love, support, and patience. Thank you, Grandmother, for shedding your last bit of light onto me. May you rest in peace. Paris, my dear friend, thanks for showing me just how thick water can be. Lastly, Deborah, thank you for your generosity, kindness, and guidance. Samuel, I love you!

I

Denial

September 25th, 2020, a bright fall morning shined through the suburbs of sunny San Francisco. Some neighbors were out for their morning exercise routine. Most would say this was the perfect neighborhood, peaceful, and quiet. As perfect as things may seem on the surface, there's always something rotting away underneath. One particular home appeared to be perfect. The grass was cut low, meeting the city standards and was surrounded by fall décor. But as neighbors got closer, the sound of ceramic glass shattering against the wall was heard as one suburban couple revealed the darkness of their marriage.

Bobby and Jasmine, both police officers and type-A personalities, have known each other since high school. Though still to this day haven't found a way to get along. Both codependent on each other more than they realized, drag out their relationship, rather than setting each other free. The sound of ceramic plates shattering against the wall continued as Jasmine tried to strike Bobby; only he continued to dodge her throws.

Instantly, Jasmine caught Bobby off guard and struck him with a dish across his face, causing him to bleed from his left eyebrow. Bobby now infuriated, rushed toward Jasmine, and slapped her across the forehead, causing her to lose balance and fall to the ground. Not having any concern for Jasmine, Bobby reached for a paper towel from the countertop and wiped his face. Both were now panting, and out of breath, Jasmine looked up at Bobby to say,

"I want a fucking divorce."

"Oh yeah, I want a million dollars, but that's not going to happen either, you will never be free from me, I own you! Do you hear me? There's no world, no fucking universe, where you exist without me."

Jasmine, irate by Bobby's reply, got up from the floor and left him standing alone in the kitchen while he babied his wound.

Just down the street, a newly married lesbian couple by the names of Veronica and Gloria live in a pleasant and inviting home. Both of them appear to have it together, or maybe it's just the honeymoon phase. Whatever it may be, things are quite steamy this morning between the two of them. Gloria and Veronica have been together for four years and married two months ago. Gloria, the more dominant of the two, was preparing breakfast when she became distracted by her wife's beauty.

Veronica walked into the kitchen half dressed wearing a laced red bra, and a blue skirt. She was drawn into the kitchen by the sweet smell of hickory-smoked bacon sizzling in the skillet. Gloria immediately approached Veronica and placed her hand on the small of Veronica's back as she pulled her close. Both Veronica and Gloria smiled at one another before they reached in for a passionate kiss.

"Tal vez deberiamo llevar esto a la habitacion, mi amor," Gloria whispered.

"Oh, yes, I love you too!" Veronica replied, and yet had no idea of what Gloria just said to her.

Veronica wrapped her arms around Gloria's neck while Gloria caressed Veronica's back squeezing her close ever so gently. The bacon began to burn in the skillet, but the smell of burnt bacon sure didn't stop them. As the bacon continued to burn on the stove, Gloria lifted Veronica onto the island countertop. Veronica then wrapped her legs around Gloria's waist, and they continued embracing one another with pleasure filled kisses. Just moments later, the fire alarm sounded off. Veronica jumped off of the countertop, and they both rushed to turn off the stove and disposed of the charcoal bacon. Gloria became upset that her surprise breakfast was destroyed, and began to shout in disappointment.

"Oh mierda, ahora el desayuno esta arruinado."

"I don't know what you're saying, baby, but it's okay...ESTOY BIEN."

Unlike most couples, Veronica and Gloria face one little dilemma in their relationship, *The Language Barrier*. Veronica then rushed to open the sliding door behind them in their kitchen, only to see a familiar face on the other side. Veronica's friend, Erika, walked inside. Veronica and Erika have a love-hate relationship. Veronica rolled her eyes after Erika barged her way inside. Fanning the smoke away from her face, Erika looked to Veronica for answers.

"What the hell happened?"

"I hope you realize that my opening the door wasn't an invitation for you to come inside."

"I see you're still mean and hateful as ever," Erika smiled and continued, "I looked over, and it seemed like you both needed help. I could hear the alarm going off from the sidewalk. What did Gloria burn this time?"

"Don't insult my wife like that," Veronica barked.

"Oh please, you two have been married all of, thirty days?"

"Sixty days!"

Veronica replied in frustration as she continued to fan the smoke out of the room. Erika, on the other hand, dismissed Veronica and began conversing with Gloria. Another quality Veronica couldn't stand about Erika was her bilingual talents. Veronica felt threatened, making her insecurities of being a good wife soar. Veronica didn't have any understanding of the Spanish language, and loathed being the only person in a room who couldn't communicate, especially with her wife. Erika continued speaking to Gloria in her native language, and Veronica grew furious.

"If you're going to speak to my wife, at my house, at least speak in a language that I can understand!"

"Wait a minute, you two have been together for four years, got married, and you still don't know Spanish! Don't you think you should have taken care of that before you two got married?"

"Get out!" Veronica shouted.

"Why, because I'm telling you the truth?"

At that moment, the alarm stopped sounding, and Veronica stared at Erika with revulsion. The room grew silent, and Erika could quickly sense that she was unwelcomed.

"Okay, I'll leave."

"Thank you!"

Erika spoke in Spanish once more as she said goodbye to Gloria, just driving the knife deeper into Veronica's spine. Erika then walked past

Veronica with a smirk and continued with her day as she walked out through the kitchen sliding door. Veronica then slammed the door shut making sure Erika could feel her fury. After taking a moment to inhale and exhale, Veronica walked over towards Gloria, who was completely confused by what just happened.

"Te quiero amo. Don't …be jealous," Gloria smiled and calmed Veronica as she kissed and embraced her gently.

On the other side of town, a woman named Nicole Howard was getting ready to leave for work. Nicole owns a small condo in downtown San Francisco at one of those fancy high-rise buildings; yes, she's that person, but not exactly. Nicole is a strong, fierce, independent woman of color who gets what she wants in life. Nicole left her apartment and took the elevator down to the lobby of her condominium. As soon as Nicole stepped off, she noticed an attractive brunette who looked as if she was either headed to a magazine shoot, or just came from one. The woman was wearing athletic shorts, a tank top, and had the legs to match. Nicole quickly became interested and approached. Not caring about or even noticing the man standing next to the woman, Nicole slyly slipped the tall beauty her business card, and boldly said,

"Whenever you get bored of him, and you will...give me a call."

Nicole used her wits and charm to get the woman's attention. However, the man standing next to her took offense, but before he could say a word, Nicole walked away with a smile heading off to work at the law firm. Being one of San Francisco's best comes with a lot of responsibility, responsibility that often requires her attention. Nicole, however, arrived late to a meeting that she had scheduled with her client. A young married couple in their mid-twenties has decided to get a divorce. Paul, the husband, caught his wife Julie, having an affair. Paul, now bitter and seeking revenge, wants not only a divorce, but also full custody of their four-year-old son, and their unborn child. Julie, who is eight months pregnant, wasn't going down without a fight. As Nicole took her seat, Paul's lawyer, greeted her with sarcasm.

"So nice of you to finally join us, Nicole."

"My apologies, you all know how San Francisco

traffic can be. Now, with that out of the way, let's get on with it, shall we?"

Nicole took her reading glasses from her briefcase, and also the paperwork she had drawn up. Nicole then placed the papers on the table for everyone to see and began to speak.

"My client has agreed to settle this case and wants nothing in return, except for shared custody of the children. Paul can keep the house, the cars..." Before Nicole could finish her thought, Paul rudely interrupted her.

"No, I don't want my kids, my newborn child around any of the strangers she decides to bring home and fuck! I want full custody; she can keep the fucking house."

Paul's slurs offended Julie as she glared over at him in shock. Paul's lawyer then began to speak,

"My client has shared his concerns, which are more than understandable. The children, once born, BOTH need stability. Going from home to home, having strangers coming and going..."

"What the hell is this about strangers coming and going? Julie grew furious and continued, "I had an affair yes, with one person, one who I've known for years. A man who has loved and taken care of me more than you ever could, Paul."

The room became quiet as Julie and Paul heated the room with their vexations. Paul's lawyer continued speaking,

"Paul has requested full custody, he is stable, and an upstanding father, and he's willing to take this to court if need be." Nicole now fed up with the direction the meeting was headed, interrupted,

"Alright, well, that's not going to happen. Men always think they can rip children away from their mothers because they have the money and power to do so. These children are not a pawn in your game, and they don't give a fuck about who wins, or who has all the goddamn power! It's clear what needs to happen and what is *going* to happen. These children will be apart of their mother's life because she is their mother! Julie is not unfit; she was trapped in a marriage, one of which she freed herself. Now, the two of you can test me all you want, but I deeply suggest you take *my* offer!" The room grew silent again, and both Paul and his lawyer backed down.

On the other side of town, at CBS studios, Veronica arrived to work to anchor the midday news as she took her place on stage. She carefully sat down and made sure not to wrinkle her skirt, or alter her clothing in any way. Veronica then took out her phone to use it as a mirror. Veronica always made sure that her hair was in place as she combed her fingers through gently. The lights then shined bright onto her milk creamy skin as the countdown was underway.

The cameraperson a few feet away set up the camera by getting Veronica in focus, then gave her a one minute time cue. Veronica acknowledged by looking up, then back down at her phone. Veronica took one last glance at herself, to make sure that her lipstick was perfect. Then suddenly, she noticed a text from Erika that read,

"I'm sorry, how many times do I have to say this, when are you going to forgive me?"

Veronica became distracted by Erika's text and almost missed her time cue to go live. Veronica quickly put her phone out of sight and positioned herself poise and confidant as the 10-second countdown went underway. Before Veronica could take a deep breath, she was cued to speak, and the music faded in.

"Good afternoon, it's Friday, September 25th,

three months after the stay at home orders have lifted across the country. Stay tuned to see what CDC officials are doing to prevent the second spread of COVID 19. I'm Veronica Rodriguez, and I'll have more on that, coming up."

Though Veronica smiled for the cameras, and her wife at home, she was feeding a grudge that was slowly eating away at her happiness.

While Veronica continued to anchor the midday news, her friend Jasmine was heading into work with her husband, Bobby. Both dressed in uniform, and both still shaken up from their morning brawl, they walked into the precinct together. Greeted by fellow officers, Jasmine and Bobby tried to hide their wounds, those visible and non-visible. Bobby had a cut above his left eye, which he applied a clear Band-Aid to cover up. Jasmine's wounds hid underneath her uniform and were easier to hide. A friendly face approached and quickly became curious.

"Damn, what the hell happened to you two? It looks like you both woke up on the wrong side of the bed, literally."

"We're fine!" Both Bobby and Jasmine replied in defense.

These two clearly have an unhealthy, abusive relationship, which they both need to free themselves from. What's more terrifying is that everyone seemed to be aware of how unhealthy Bobby and Jasmine's relationship was, except for them. The denial caused Bobby and Jasmine to continue their cycle of abuse and codependency. The unfortunate, sad truth of the matter is that it was easier for them to stay together, rather than facing the hard truth and leaving. Jasmine pretended that everything was fine as she headed to her desk. Bobby watched Jasmine walk away, but wasn't able to wear a poker face as well as she was. Bobby's good friend, and fellow officer, continued to pry.

"Dude, what the hell happened?" Bobby walked away to his desk, but his friend followed. Bobby began to fiddle with the bunch of papers that were on top of his desk.

"Are you just going to keep following me, man? I don't know what you're talking about."

"I'm talking about your face? You don't think that people know what goes on between you two?"

"There is nothing going on; I got scratched this morning...by a cat."

"Yeah, a feisty cat named Jasmine." Bobby began to stare down his friend in frustration, but he only continued to pry.

"Listen, man, when are you guys going to get some professional help?"

"We don't need professional help, we're fine."

Denial, it's the ugly devil that lives in us all. Eventually, we are all faced with taking it head-on and striking it out, discovering the truth that's hidden away underneath. Like Erika, for example, she arrived for a therapy appointment later that day. Erika checked in at the front desk and took a seat as she waited for her therapist to call her back. As Erika sat there twiddling her thumbs, she nervously watched the people who were also in the lobby. Moments passed, and eventually, Erika's therapist was ready to see her. Greeted with a smile and a warm hug, Erika embraced her therapist and smiled back.

They proceeded to walk to her office, and once inside, Erika felt an immediate calming. The office had art decorated on every wall, and therapeutic candles burned on the desk. Erika's therapist knew how to make her patients feel at ease. Erika then sat on the bright blue sofa, and her therapist began to speak.

"So Erika, how has this past week treated you? Did you do anything new or exciting?"

"In the past week, no. Not really, how about you?"

"Well, my niece, the five-year-old that I told you about, she got a new cat. Now she has a total of four cats!"

"Wow!" Erika replied in an edgy manner, and her therapist continued to speak, "I can barely keep up with one!" The two of them began to chuckle at the idea of a child having four cats, and Erika's therapist went on to say,

"Another exciting thing that happened was, I tried a new Thai food restaurant. Awesome place, called, Boon Mee, you should try it!"

"Hm, maybe I will someday." Erika's responses were mostly dry, but she tried her best to seem interested.

"You're supposed to try something new every week whether it's trying a new restaurant, exploring a new area, or even adopting a pet. Why haven't you tried this exercise? It's been four weeks in a row."

"And I always tell you that I don't have time. Being the owner of a bar takes up a lot of my day. I especially don't have time for pets."

"Why don't you make time for yourself? You make time for work, for your responsibilities, but you don't make any time for yourself to find joy."

"Honestly, there's nothing for me to be joyful about."

Erika felt as though everyone else around her was doing better, succeeding, and thriving. Worst of all, Erika felt as though she didn't have love in her life. Although she was a complete annoyance to Veronica earlier as she often is, it wasn't because she wants to be that way, but instead, it's her defense mechanism. A couple of years ago, Veronica and her now-wife, Gloria, got into a nasty fight. Of course, Erika was there to pick up the pieces, but not for Veronica. Erika allowed herself to break her sisterly bond with Veronica by abusing and misusing her trust, all to satisfy her emptiness for love. Erika didn't realize that she would lose a best friend in the process.

"Why do you believe there's nothing for you to be joyful about?"

"The one thing I want more than anything else in the world, I'll never have. My friends, they are complete, especially my friend Nicole. Women flock to her as soon as she steps into a room. But me, I struggle to find one person to even look my way."

"I thought you were in a relationship with someone, did that end?"

"Not yet, but...I suspect that my girlfriend is cheating," Erika replied with uncertainty.

"Why do you think that?"

"It's a woman's intuition. Something's just different, off."

"You don't think she loves you?"

"I know that she doesn't. There's not a single person on this planet who loves me."

Erika began to whimper. She hid behind her tough exterior when all she wanted was to be happy.

"What about your mother, she loved you."

"My mother is dead. That doesn't help me now, does it? The only people I have left in my life are you and my 2.5 friends."

"Why do you say that?"

"Veronica, the one I told you about, she's never going to forgive me. She hates my guts."

"Have you acknowledged your actions, and sincerely apologized?"

"I apologized many times. I don't get how she could cut me off completely; she and Gloria weren't even together for long at the time."

"I hear you, but it doesn't sound like you're taking any responsibility. You use the fact that Veronica and Gloria weren't in a relationship for long as a way to make your actions okay."

"She doesn't know what happened, only what I told her," Erika replied in defense.

"For you to offer a sincere apology, you must first own your actions. Whatever happened, it was serious enough to cost you your friendship. You are in control of your actions, not others. You keep finding ways to justify your behavior by punishing those around you who have things you don't have. Focus on what you do have, and how you can use it positively."

Erika tried to heed her therapist's advice but instead continued to focus on the negative in her life. Erika fed the darkness inside because it was easier than doing the work to break down those self-destructive patterns. Erika didn't realize that working on one's self takes discipline, time, and patience. Erika wanted things to go her way, to be handed to her. She felt the world owed her that much, since it left her without a family, without love, as she put it. Erika was speeding up the ticking time bomb inside, and if not careful, would go off in a way that she isn't ready for.

On a brighter note, Mr. Howard, *Daniel*, a high school Astronomy teacher, ended his day giving the class a lesson on quantum physics. His students loved him. Daniel was the kind of teacher students could joke around with, and also challenge. Daniel reminded most people of a young, physically fit version of Santa Clause because of his full blonde beard and rosy cheeks. The room filled with about twenty-five students eagerly listening, while Daniel passionately talked about his multiverse theories. Before being a high school teacher, Daniel was on his way to being one of the world's greatest astrologists, at least that how he liked to put it. His dream fell apart when he had a car accident and broke his leg. Daniel couldn't finish his last year of schooling due to physical therapy.

TWO TRUTHS AND A LIE THAT SET ME FREE

When Daniel married, he became content with his life as a stay at home dad. Daniel feared to start over, worried that he wouldn't be able to commit to a life of astronomy. So, Daniel chose the next best thing, teaching.

"Who here believes in the multiverse theory?"

The room stood quiet as the students looked up with curiosity.

"What if I were to tell you that there's more just beyond the multiverse? That the universes are big bubbles inside an even bigger bubble?"

"I'd say that we're all robots in a place like *Westworld*, and we are all controlled by a superhuman," one young student replied.

"You mean God?" Another student replied.

"Alright, I see you all have your theories. That's the beautiful thing about life; there are endless possibilities and theories out there. I want you all to go home, write a single page essay of your theories, and have it ready for the next class."

The bell sounded off, and the students rushed out, anxious for the day to be over. Not a single student was in the room by the time Daniel walked over toward his desk and grabbed his bag. Ms.

Brown, the math teacher across the way, walked inside and greeted him.

"Hey Daniel, I heard you bringing out your inner, Neal DeGrasse Tyson," Ms. Brown said as she batted her bright blue eyes, and smiled.

"Yeah, It's difficult for me not to be passionate about astronomy. How are things going in math class, are the students giving you any trouble?"

"No, not really. You know kids will be kids, especially at this age."

Ms. Brown had an obvious crush on Daniel, and would often hit on him. At times, she believed it was reciprocated; but Daniel was very polite and too timid to say otherwise. Though it did seem as if Daniel liked the attention, the same attention he lacked from his wife at home. He stood still while Ms. Brown continued to flirt and took a step closer.

"You know, I believe in the multiverse theory too. I believe that sometimes, the people we marry are like place holders. We aren't supposed to be with them for eternity, but for a season, just long enough to mold our minds and souls, so that when our true love walks through the door, we will be ready."

Daniel became speechless as he reached for his jacket, which he placed over his chair.

"Well I must go, my kids are waiting for me to pick them up from school today, uh see you tomorrow?" Daniel awkwardly squeezed passed Ms. Brown and walked towards the door, leaving her standing alone in the classroom.

"Yeah, see you tomorrow, she smiled."

Daniel then rushed to pick his kids up from school. With their school being just down the street, it didn't take long for him to arrive. Daniel pulled up to the side of the curb to see his eight-year-old twins, Jeremiah and Ruth, fiddling around, waiting near the driveway on the sidewalk. Daniel parked, got out, and gave them both a big bear hug.

"Hey kids, how was school?"

"Good. I made a duck in art class today, see daddy?" Ruth said eagerly.

Daniel reached down, picked up the duck, which she made out of newspaper, and said,

"Wow, you did this all by yourself?"

"Yes!" She replied with a giant smile.

"I wonder where you get all this talent from."

Daniel was so proud to be a father as he reached

over and kissed Ruth on her forehead. Jeremiah, on the other hand, felt left out as he stared up at his father.

"What about me? I dissected a cow's eyeball."

"A cow's eyeball?" Daniel said with confusion and curiosity.

"Yeah, it was squishy, and smelt like ass."

Daniel was immediately shocked by the word Jeremiah used.

"Where did you learn that word from?"

"Mommy!"

"Mommy, huh, we need to give mommy a call."

Daniel escorted Jeremiah and Ruth into the car and began to drive off. The kids loved it when their dad picked them up because he had a brand new tesla. It kept the children busy while they played games in the back seat. Daniel placed a call to his wife and eagerly waited for her to pick up. Nicole was in her office finishing up last-minute paperwork on the computer. Nicole looked down at her desk and noticed her cell phone vibrating and immediately answered the call.

"Hi kids, are you being good?"

"Yes," Both replied.

"Jeremiah, why don't you tell mommy about that new word you learned?"

"What new word?" Nicole asked with curiosity.

"Ass?" Jeremiah shouted, wondering what the fuss was about.

"Jeremiah! Where did you learn that word from, your daddy?"

"Yes," Jeremiah smiled as he stared at his dad in the rearview mirror.

"What, you told me you learned it from mommy, remember?"

"No, Daniel, he did not learn that from me."

Nicole and Daniel go back and forth about where or whom Jeremiah may have learned that lousy word from but have yet to remind him not to use it. The topic eventually died down, and Daniel asked Nicole if she would be home for dinner. Not knowing that Nicole has been living a double life, dating, or let's be real, sleeping with other women, Daniel waited for a reply.

"I'm working on it, I just have a few things to finish up here, and I will be home. What's for dinner?"

"I was thinking of making spaghetti. How does that sound, kids?"

"Yay, spaghetti," Jeremiah and Ruth shouted with excitement.

"Well, spaghetti, it is," Daniel smiled.

"Perfect, I'll see you all soon."

"Okay, honey, we love you."

"I love you guys too! Be good and no more bad language Jeremiah."

Nicole smiled as she hung up the phone. Moments later, Nicole's secretary informed her that someone named Lisa arrived to see her. Nicole was confused, as she wasn't expecting a guest. Her secretary then went on to convey that Lisa received her business card earlier that morning. It took Nicole a minute to remember the encounter, and she then allowed her secretary to send Lisa over. Nicole quickly got herself together, making sure there weren't any visible flaws showing before Lisa walked inside. Nicole tried to play it cool as she calmly sat back in her seat, waiting for Lisa to approach the door with a smile. Nicole then straightened herself in her seat and said,

"Hi, Lisa, is it?"

"Yes, hi! Sorry to barge in on you. I just assumed that when you gave me your business card, you wanted me to use it. Plus, it was pretty bold of you to flirt with me in front of my boyfriend. You got me curious."

"Curious?" Nicole asked with a smile.

"Actually, you uh...turned me on."

Nicole smiled at Lisa and watched as she stood by the door biting her bottom lip

Nicole then got up, walked toward Lisa, and stood just inches away. She then gently grabbed Lisa's hand and placed it in hers. The two women exchanged smiles, and Nicole slowly closed the door behind them. While Nicole was beginning to satisfy her appetite, Jasmine and Bobby were investigating a missing person case. A man accused of kidnapping sat in the interrogation room opposite of Officer Smith, Bobby. Bobby tried to coerce the truth out of the suspect. However, this suspect was more on the stubborn side than he realized.

As the suspect sat in the chair with ripped clothing, long uneven beard, and eyes that looked of death, Jasmine watched from the two-way mirror and quickly became furious by his non-responsiveness. Jasmine stormed her way into the interrogation room, grabbed the gentleman by the collar, and pointed her gun to the side of his forehead, demanding an answer.

"We don't have time for the bullshit! That little girl is going to die if you don't open your goddamn mouth and talk. And at this point, I don't care about losing my job. I will paint the wall behind you with what's left of that brain inside your skull if you don't tell us everything we need to know, NOW!"

Bobby sat from across the table, shocked by Jasmine's actions. Though her behavior may have been extreme, and against her job policy, she was able to get the necessary information. About 30 minutes later, the officers were able to locate the missing child buried under rubbish in the woods near a creek. If the officers didn't get to the little girl when they did, she might not have survived. Jasmine and Bobby were both on the crime scene, engaging in small talk. Though Bobby seemed to have dusted off this morning's fight and tucked it away in a dark corner of his mind, Jasmine remembered every detail and has started to become fed up with their cycle of behavior.

Their lieutenant immediately approached Jasmine about her stunt in the interrogation room. Lieutenant Grant often wore a frown, short and stout, and began to question Jasmine. Bobby backed away, giving her space to explain her actions.

"I know that I was out of line back there, I've just been under a lot of pressure lately."

"I can tell, listen, you know there are programs out here for you...for people in your situation," Lieutenant Grant replied.

"I don't know what you mean."

"Your marriage, it's affecting you more than you realize. And yes, today you saved a little girl, but when are you going to save yourself?"

Jasmine held her composer as she tried to keep herself from falling apart. Jasmine began to realize that she needed to make a change in her life. Lieutenant Grant watched Bobby as he stood further away with the other officers. Lieutenant Grant then reached into his pocket and handed Jasmine a business card with a number on it.

"You should give them a call; there's someone there who could help you, maybe even both of you. But you cannot pull anything like that again, you hear?"

"Yes, sir, it won't happen again."

"I see big things for you, hell you could even be a Lieutenant one day, but you have to take care of yourself first." Lieutenant Grant walked away, leaving Jasmine with a few thoughts.

As they wrapped things up at the crime scene, Erika was preparing for her date with her girlfriend, Evangeline. The two of them have been together for about six months, but Erika was starting to believe that history was repeating itself. Erika hasn't had the best luck in the love department, but she continued to open her heart to more pain. Erika sat patiently at a table in a fancy restaurant, the same place her therapist referred earlier. Candles lit the room, and booths. Erika took a deep breath and checked her watched. Time passed as she waited for her date to arrive. A few more moments passed, and Erika began to grow impatient. Before she could get up to leave, Evangeline rushed in with sweat dripping off of her face. She stated it was the weather, and that she had some last minute running around to do.

Evangeline apologized as she flopped into her seat, but Erika was too skeptical to believe her words. Evangeline then fanned herself, revealing a mark on the side of her neck. Erika focused on the spot, but before she could question it, the waitress arrived with water and menus. Both Erika and Evangeline informed the waitress that they would need more time before placing their order. As soon as the waitress walked away, Erika began interrogating Evangeline.

"What's that?"

"What's what, babe?"

"Don't play stupid, that mark on your neck?" Erika replied,

"Babe, calm down, it's probably just a pimple or my allergies."

At that moment, Erika began to feel as though Evangeline was not only cheating but did not respect her enough, to be honest. Respect was crucial to Erika, especially in her relationships. Erika spent time and money into spoiling Evangeline by bringing her to one of the most expensive restaurants in San Francisco, but quickly started to regret that decision.

"So tell me, how was your day?" Evangeline asked as she tried to change the subject.

"Well, a couple of my employees at the bar thought they could get over, and steal from me. They thought I wouldn't notice. It's frustrating how people continue to take my kindness for weakness, how people can lie right to my face, and not even bat an eye."

Erika referred to Evangeline as she gave her a dirty stare. The waitress arrived with wine and poured the women a glass. The waitress waited for the two of them to place their orders, but Evangeline began to feel threatened by Erika and asked for another moment. After the waitress walked away again, Evangeline glared at Erika and said,

"Are you calling me a liar now?"

"I don't know? Is there something that you need to tell me?"

"I'm not going to do this with you. I tried to have a nice peaceful dinner with you and…"

"Did you! Because it looks to me like you just got done having sex with someone else."

"You know what, since you want to throw around all these false accusations, I'm leaving. Enjoy your dinner."

"I reserved this fucking table; I can't get my money back."

"You should have thought about that before you came at me with all your insecurities."

Evangeline rushed up from the table, and Erika followed behind, causing a scene while the people inside gawked. Evangeline swung the door open, and Erika followed her outside. Evangeline then rushed to her vehicle, which was parked just down the street. Erika noticed Evangeline checking her phone on the way, and instantly became jealous.

"Give me your phone," Erika shouted.

"No! You're out of control."

Evangeline tried to hide her phone from Erika as she rushed inside her vehicle. Erika hurried to open the passenger side door before Evangeline could lock her out. Erika then sat in the passenger seat and continued to reach for Evangeline's phone. The more of a fight Evangeline put up, the more sinister Erika became. Evangeline tried to kick Erika out of her car by shoving her out with her body. Consumed with anger and betrayal, Erika reached over, swung her body on top of Evangeline's, grabbed her by the neck, and squeezed tightly. Slowly losing her breath, Evangeline fought for her life as she tried to loosen Erika's grip by prying her fingers open. Erika only squeezed tighter.

Her soul became nothing but darkness as her eyes filled with blackness, and her teeth looked like that of a monster as she clinched tight to

Evangeline's neck. Erika felt a high, a sense of satisfaction watching Evangeline squirm and turn from red to blue. Evangeline slowly lost what little fight she had left, and as her body relaxed, her soul slowly faded away. Erika then released her hold, and flopped back into the passenger seat, panting and sweating while staring back at Evangeline. A minute passed before Erika came to and attempted to wake Evangeline.

"Wake up!"

Erika poked at Evangeline's body and quickly became aware that she was sitting next to a corpse. Erika became hysterical and noticed an audience staring back at her through the window of the car. An older gentleman and his wife stared in confusion. Erika was too consumed with anger, jealousy, and betrayal to consider her actions and the consequence. Now fully aware, Erika slowly stepped out of the vehicle, and walked away distraught, leaving Evangeline's body decaying away. It was only a matter of time before her transgressions would catch up with her.

While Erika was getting more and more unlucky in life, Nicole was getting away with another affair. Nicole may seem like a monster for her choices, but she was dealt an unfair hand in life. She could either choose herself and her happiness or her husband and the kids. Nicole decided long ago that she wasn't going to choose between the two. Nicole and Lisa sat together, half-dressed on the carpeted floor in her office. Fanning themselves from the sweat they've built up, they began to engage in conversation.

"I'm glad you decided to come by, instead of calling," Nicole said with a smile.

"I'm glad I did too!"

"So, what are you going to do about that boyfriend of yours?" Nicole whispered.

"Hm, I haven't thought about him, what do you think I should do?"

"I think you should get rid of him," Nicole and Lisa both chuckled.

Nicole then got up from the floor, turned on the television in her office, and began dressing. Channel 5 News was airing, and Nicole became shocked by what she saw. The news showed a reporter at the scene where Evangeline was murdered. Paramedics arrived, and took Evangeline's body out of her vehicle, then placed it on a stretcher. A photo of Erika appeared on the news as a possible suspect.

Nicole stared in silence and puzzlement. Lisa then got up and began dressing while she watched the news with Nicole.

"That's just horrible. Do you know that woman?"

"Yeah, unfortunately, I do."

Nicole continued getting dressed until she heard a knock at the door. Nicole then rushed to put on the rest of her clothes and motioned for Lisa to follow suit.

"One minute!" Nicole checked her hair, face, and teeth to make sure she was presentable and opened the door to see her secretary on the other side.

"Yes?" Nicole asked.

"You have another visitor."

Erika approached from behind and walked inside, distraught and in tears. Lisa quickly recognized Erika from the photo displayed on the news. She then grabbed her things and gave Nicole back her business card with her number written on it. Nicole took Lisa's number and hugged her goodbye. Both Lisa and the secretary exited her office, and Nicole quickly closed the door behind them.

"Please, please tell me you didn't have anything to do with what I just saw on the news."

"I need a lawyer."

"Damn it!" Erika took a seat and almost missed the chair due to her disorientation. Nicole pulled up a chair and sat next to her.

"Erika, you know that I cannot represent you."

"You can't, or you don't want to? I don't have anyone else! Nobody will give a damn about what happens to me. Please, you're all I've got."

Before Nicole could say another word, her secretary interrupted her again. Veronica barged her way inside Nicole's office, not paying any mind to her secretary. Once inside, Veronica was surprised to see that Erika already beat her there.

"I'm sorry, Mrs. Howard, I tried to stop her!"

"It's okay; we obviously have a lot to discuss."

"Okay, well, I'm going to take off, you all have a great night."

"Thanks, you too," Nicole awkwardly smiled.

Nicole, Erika, and Veronica waited for her secretary to leave the office. Once Nicole noticed that her secretary had packed up for the day, she shut the door and glared over at Erika.

"You better have a good explanation for this."

"It was an accident."

"An accident? How is choking someone to death an accident?" Veronica interrupted.

"Veronica!" Nicole shouted.

"What!" Veronica yelled back.

"It's only going to be a matter of time before the police piece this together. Your picture is on the goddamn news as a suspect for crying out loud. I don't know what I can do," Nicole said.

"I need your help! I need your help," Erika stood up and pleaded.

Nicole took a moment to consider representing Erika while Veronica shook her head in disapproval. Nicole has been a very successful lawyer for the past twelve years and has yet to lose a case. Nicole feared that taking Erika's case would not only change her A-plus track record but ruin her friendship as well. Veronica stared at Erika with judgment and asked,

"Erika, why did you do this? What did Evangeline do to you that was so upsetting, you felt like you needed to kill her?"

"Do not judge me! Don't! I don't know why I did it, I just did. I wasn't mentally right."

"Here we go again, playing the mentally ill card," Veronica interrupted.

"Fuck you," Erika shouted.

"No, Fuck you! You are so fucking spoiled; you think your actions don't have any consequences. You're not mentally ill; you're crazy."

"Alright that's enough, stop it! You're both acting like children," Nicole shouted.

Veronica immediately became offended by Nicole comparing her to a child while staring at her with her arms folded in a childlike manner. At that moment, Nicole decided to help her friend. She believed that Erika wouldn't stand a chance without her. Nicole explained that Erika should turn herself in, or allow the police to bring her in. Erika didn't agree; she suggested hiding out until she could gather her thoughts.

"So wait, now you want us to be accomplices in your murder so you can have some time to think? I'm not going to jail for you," Veronica shouted.

"I just need...some time," Erika replied.

"You can ride with me to my house, give yourself some time to process everything. But, when the police come, and they will, it would be wise if you didn't run."

"You're making a mistake by helping her. She

doesn't care about anyone but herself or who she has to hurt along the way."

Veronica rushed out of the room, leaving Nicole and Erika standing alone. Erika turned toward Nicole and thanked her.

"Don't thank me; I haven't saved your ass yet," Nicole checked her watch. "And now, I'm late for dinner, Daniel's cooking spaghetti tonight." Nicole grabbed her things, and as she got ready to head out, Erika became curious.

"Who was that woman?"

"Honestly, right now, at this moment, my personal life should be the least of your concerns." Nicole then stood by the door and motioned for Erika to walk through.

While on the way to Nicole and Daniel's house, Mrs. Howard prepared Erika for what should happen once the police arrive. Knowing that it was only a matter of time before they'd show up, Nicole made it clear just how important it was that she didn't speak a word. Nicole then insisted on using the insanity plea. But Erika quickly became offended by that idea.

"I'm not fucking insane."

"Do you want to spend the rest of your life in

prison? I've never lost a case, and I don't intend to start now."

Nicole finally arrived home and pulled into the driveway. They both sat in the car for a moment before walking inside.

"We have a little bit of time. But you need to know; It doesn't matter what you think, it matters what you can convince the jury to believe," Nicole whispered.

"I hope you're right," Erika agreed, and they both got out of the vehicle. Erika nervously looked over her shoulder as she rushed behind Nicole. Once inside, Jeremiah and Ruth welcomed their mother.

"Mommy, mommy," They both shouted for joy as they surround her with hugs.

"Mom, what took you so long?" Ruth eagerly asked.

"Mommy had to take care of a few things, but I'm home now. Listen, why don't you both get ready for dinner. I need to talk to your dad." They heeded their mother's request and rushed to get ready for dinner. Erika slowly stepped out from behind Nicole, and Daniel approached greeting the two of them but noticed something strange in Erika's body language.

"Is everything okay?" Daniel asked with concern.

"Daniel listen, the police will be here any moment. I need you to keep the kids occupied." Nicole pleaded.

"The police, what's going on?"

"Please, Daniel? I don't want the kids to know about any of this, I will explain later." Daniel agreed, and then rushed off after the kids, taking Nicole's concern more serious. Nicole waited with Erika in the living room for the police to arrive. Knowing that their friend was a police officer, Nicole had a feeling they would be searching for Erika in one of three places; her place was one of them. In the near distance, police lights shined bright, and sirens grew louder. Nicole and Erika could see the blue and red lights shining through the curtains in the living room. Nicole stood with Erika by the door and held her hand for comfort.

"Are you ready?" Nicole asked.

"Do I have a choice?"

Suddenly, there was a knock at the door that startled them both. Nicole walked closer toward the door, took a deep breath, then turned the knob slowly as she opened, only to see Jasmine standing on the other side with a crew of officers.

"You know that I hate what I'm about to do, right?" Jasmine said to Nicole and glanced over at Erika.

"I know." Nicole stepped aside and allowed Jasmine and the other officers to walk inside. Jasmine's heart broke when she saw Erika standing there looking horrified.

"What happened?" Jasmine whispered to Erika with concern.

"Just do it."

Erika surrendered, and Jasmine paused before placing her under arrest. Jasmine proceeded to escort Erika outside of Nicole's home in handcuffs, but before she walked out, Jasmine whispered to Nicole,

"What the hell happened?"

Nicole shrugged her shoulders in confusion and didn't say a word. Jasmine then continued to escort Erika out of the home, and the other officers followed behind. Nicole watched as the officers left her home and placed Erika into the police vehicle. As quickly as Nicole's home filled up, it just as quickly emptied. She was left standing by the door in silence with her thoughts.

Veronica was at home, panicking, pacing near the foot of the bed. Gloria sat patiently on top of the bed as she watched, trying to figure out what was wrong with Veronica. Gloria tried her best to read Veronica's lips and make out individual words that she may recognize. With Veronica yelling a mile a minute, the only thing Gloria could do was appear empathic until she could speak.

"I mean, what the fuck! I'm just extremely confused. I knew the woman was insane, but I didn't believe she was actually INSANE, not until today."

"¿Qué?" Gloria asked.

"I don't know; I don't even know how this could happen. I get it; I shouldn't judge, but..."

"¿Qué?" Gloria was still confused and didn't understand a single word that Veronica uttered. Veronica became agitated even more as she tried to explain.

"Oh my God! Did you not understand a word that I just said? I sometimes forget that your

English is poor. I guess I'll have to get out Google translator, again..."

Veronica huffed and puffed as she flopped down on the bed next to Gloria. Gloria noticed Veronica using her phone to translate, and she reached for her phone as well. Veronica read aloud as she typed in Google.

"My...friend...was...arrested...for...killing...her...girlfriend."

Veronica translated and showed Gloria her phone with the translated message. Gloria's eyes became wide like gumballs, and she began to freak out.

"QUE! Jasmine? Sabia que iba a suceder uno de estos dias!"

"What, no! Not Jasmine, Erika!"

"Erika?" Gloria asked with confusion. Veronica inhaled and exhaled in frustration.

She wished communication between them could be more accessible, and that she could rant without having to translate or explain every word. Yet, Veronica didn't make any attempts to study the Spanish language. Instead, she blamed the lack of communication on Gloria, without acknowledging her own faults.

"I'm telling you, our relationship has to be the test of true love. Because this, having to translate every single thing, every single time. I just want to be able to tell you something the first time, and you get it!"

"¿Qué?" Gloria continued to stare in confusion but remained empathic.

"Uno minute!" Veronica said as she used Google translator again.

"This time, I'm just going to translate everything at once." Veronica took a minute to translate all of her thoughts as she sped through Google translator, and corrected typos.

Veronica finished translating and had a lengthy paragraph for Gloria to read. As Gloria read, she became confused, and then had a moment of clarity. Gloria finally understood what Veronica had been trying to tell her.

"Oh no, I'm sorry, honey." Gloria then used her translator to write a message for Veronica. After another minute of typing and correcting typos, Gloria showed Veronica her phone. As Veronica read, she became emotional, and a tear dripped down her face. Relieved that Gloria finally understood, Veronica looked up at Gloria and kissed her on the cheek. Gloria then embraced Veronica as she wrapped her arm over her shoulder and held tight.

"That's why I love you so much!" Veronica whispered as she rested her head on Gloria's bosom.

"Yo También te quiero," Gloria smiled.

Back at the precinct, Jasmine requested to speak with Erika. Erika sat in the interrogation room alone, nervous, and confused. Jasmine looked through the two-way mirror and demanded that the officers turn off the sound to allow them a moment of privacy. Jasmine walked inside and sat across from Erika.

"Erika, I know Nicole may have told you not to say anything, I just…I just want to know that you're okay, mentally." Erika looked at Jasmine, wishing she could say something, but she was afraid that she would only make things worse if she did.

"Okay, well, I love you, and I'm here for you. I'm not judging you."

Jasmine got up as she tried to keep her composure and not break down. Erika fought back tears as she watched Jasmine walk out of the room. The love Jasmine offered moved Erika, more than she had been moved in years. After all, they were friends first before Nicole and Veronica were in the picture. Those simple words, I love you, was just what Erika needed to hear. The night turned to day, and Nicole dropped her twins off at school. Before Nicole released them, she had a few words,

"Alright kids, I want you to remember that I love you! Always remember to do what's right, even if it's hard or scary. If you ever have something that's bothering you, come to your dad, your teachers, or me. Never keep it inside. Do you understand?"

"Yes," Jeremiah and Ruth both replied.

"Did we do something bad?" Ruth questioned her mother.

"No...at least not that I know. I want to make sure that you both always feel like you can come to me. Okay, now give me a hug! I don't want you to be late."

Nicole hugged her kids tightly and then kissed them both on the cheek. After she released them, they waved goodbye and ran off for the start of their day. Nicole looked over and noticed a familiar face in the distance.

"Nicole? I thought that was you," Lisa approached as she caught Nicole off guard.

"Oh, hi. What are you doing here? Do you have kids?"

"No, I was just dropping off my niece, and I saw you. I didn't know that you had kids."

"Yes, two!" Nicole awkwardly replied.

"They're adorable. I like how you keep their hair so long and curly. Listen, I was on my way to grab a coffee, would you like to join? It's on me."

"Thanks but, I don't know, I have some things I need to finish up." Nicole tried to find a reason to get out of having coffee with Lisa and before she could walk away, Lisa said,

"Really? You can't spare ten minutes over a cup of coffee in public?"

"Fine, I guess it wouldn't hurt."

"Great, just follow me, I'm in the car over there." Lisa pointed to her vehicle up ahead, allowing Nicole an opportunity to identify it.

"Okay got it, I'll see you there."

When Lisa and Nicole arrived at the coffee shop, they both walked inside and ordered tall vanilla Lattes and took a seat when their drinks were ready. Lisa, full of questions, began her 21 questions game.

"So, I'm assuming that since you have kids, you are married too?" Nicole took a large gulp of her coffee before answering Lisa's question.

"Yes...yes, I'm married, unfortunately."

"Unfortunately?"

"Listen, I want to apologize, I didn't want this to turn into anything. I usually find a woman I'm attracted to, we have great sex, and we never hear from each other again."

"Wow! I feel so special," Lisa sarcastically replied.

"I'm sorry. It's just, I'm married and finding someone, a woman, I just know that's impossible."

"Why is that impossible?"

"Because, who wants to take on someone else's kids? I would have to start all over with someone new. The chances of that relationship ending before it gets started seems more likely than anything else."

"Are you happy?"

"Why does everyone ask that question?"

"I'm just curious, I mean, why would you spend

your life with someone you're not happy with, just because you're afraid to put yourself out there?"

Nicole became silent as she reflected on Lisa's comment. Reminiscing on the many times she's tried to communicate with Daniel about how she felt, wanting to date other people, women, to be exact. Nicole began to realize; she couldn't lie to herself any longer.

"What exactly are you saying?" Nicole asked.

"People have these beliefs that they religiously stand by. If I'm married and have kids, I must stay, for the kids. But it's never just about the kids. It's because people like you are afraid to do the work that it takes to start over. It's easier to stay with someone you're familiar with, instead of putting in the work to be with someone you're *supposed* to be with."

"Wait a minute, I've told my husband numerous times that I'm attracted to women. I've even asked him for a break, to date other people. He agrees for all of 10 minutes and then acts as if the conversation never happened. I've honestly just gotten used to being in a non-emotional and non-physical marriage." Nicole took a deep breath as she became frustrated by the topic.

"That is truly heartbreaking." Lisa passed judgment on Nicole, although she tried not to, she couldn't help but feel like Nicole was making excuses to stay in her marriage.

While Lisa and Nicole continued their conversation, Jasmine and Bobby were getting ready for work. Jasmine stood by the dresser, and Bobby approached with concern over her friend, Erika.

"So, how do you think she's doing in there?"

"Not good, I'm sure. You know that could easily be one of us, and it still might be," Jasmine said with concern.

"No, no. We would never take it that far." Bobby continued getting dressed, then walked into the bathroom, leaving Jasmine disturbed by his statement. She then followed behind and said,

"That's my point. We shouldn't be taking it anywhere. How did we get here?"

"It's not a question of how, but when. Jay, we've always had problems."

"We were not always physical, Jasmine sighed."

Bobby then walked back into the bedroom, and Jasmine followed once more.

"No, Jay, *we* weren't." Bobby replied."

"What's that supposed to mean? We weren't? I

was never abusive towards you, the way that you are to me. And even if I was, do you actually believe it would justify the shit you do?" Jasmine replied in frustration.

The issue with Bobby and Jasmine is that they are both in denial about their actions towards one another. Neither one of them wants to admit fault, but both are quick to blame the other. Abuse of any kind is unhealthy period. However, Bobby believes that because Jasmine strikes him on occasion, or sometimes becomes emotionally abusive, that his actions are justified. Bobby doesn't realize that when he becomes abusive, he's doing permanent damage to Jasmine's body. As Jasmine gets older, her body isn't able to sustain the blows that she was once able to heal from quickly.

"So, it's okay for you to attack me, and because I'm a man, I'm just supposed to sit around and take it? That's what you think? You wanna know what I think? If you're woman enough to put your hands on me, you're woman enough to get hit back."

Jasmine was outraged by Bobby's words and began to realize that a change needed to happen and fast. Time passed for Lisa and Nicole as they continued their conversation at the coffee shop.

Though Lisa wasn't finished with her 21 questions, Nicole wasn't ready to admit to the truth that burned inside.

"So, who was it?" Lisa asked with curiosity.

"Who?" Nicole asked in confusion.

"The woman that broke your heart." Nicole, shocked by Lisa's question, stared back at her and quickly took a sip of her coffee to avoid giving an answer.

"Come on, anyone who uses one nightstands as an escape from their marriage, there's got to be a broken heart behind it…who was she?"

Nicole took a deep breath and gently placed her cup on the table.

"She was my first…love. We met at a time when I wasn't ready to explore my sexuality. I ended things before they had a chance to blossom, and I've been with Daniel ever since. But, I felt things with her that I've never felt with anyone else, not even my husband. I've tried, really tried to tell myself that maybe in time things will change. That maybe I would have those same feelings for him, but I never do."

"Wow, that's sad." Lisa replied.

"No, it's…it's okay, I do what I have to do, you

know?" Nicole smiled in denial, and Lisa stared in shock by her reply.

"I just have one question, and don't take offense, but when your children become adults, would you want them to stay in a marriage because it's what they have to do, or because it's what they want to do?" Nicole took a moment to consider Lisa's point as she stared into thought.

Back at the Smith's home, Jasmine and Bobby finished getting ready and headed downstairs into the kitchen while continuing their conversation.

"You're in denial, and you're the one who doesn't want to take any responsibility for his actions. Yes, I may have smacked you, pushed you, and threw a dish at you, but I don't leave bruises all over your body. A man should never put his hands on a woman."

"Oh, so men are just supposed to sit around and be punching bags because yall's period came on a Tuesday? I don't get you. Why is it okay for you to put your hands on me, why is it okay for you to embarrass me, and call me names?"

"You're in denial, and it's pathetic." Jasmine said with disappointment in her eyes.

"No you're in denial, lost overseas or some shit."

"Bobby, I can't keep doing this, it's exhausting. We need professional help, because if things don't change at this point... I'm leaving."

Jasmine looked as exhausted as she sounded while she bent over the counter with her head buried in her hands. Bobby grabbed an apple from the countertop and walked over toward Jasmine to say,

"Do what you have to, I'm not going to therapy."

Bobby challenged Jasmine out of his own fears. Hoping Jasmine would back down, change her mind; he walked out of the room and headed off to work. Jasmine was left alone distraught as she stood up straight, wiping a tear from the side of her face, and left for work behind him.

Later on that morning, Nicole headed into court for Erika's arraignment. Nicole coached Erika beforehand, reminding her of what she would need to say. Nicole walked inside and noticed Erika sitting at the defense table and approached. Erika grew more nervous as she waited for the judge. Her hands became sweaty, and her skin lost its glow. Erika slumped in her seat and held her head down. Nicole noticed and tried to coach her once more as she took a seat.

"Erika, are you okay?" Erika was non-responsive to Nicole and continued to slump with her head down.

"Listen, you need to sit up, straighten your back, and try not to look so damn guilty,"

Nicole whispered sternly. Erika then slowly sat up and picked her head up when she heard the judge walking into the room. The judge took his seat at the bench, and the bailiff then ordered everyone to rise. Erika, half mentally present, didn't stand up until Nicole motioned for her to do so. Erika stood with a hunched back and continued to hold her head down. Her body then began to quiver, and Nicole noticed a steady decline in Erika's behavior.

"Stop it!" Nicole sternly whispered through her teeth. Everyone in the room then took their seats while Nicole continued standing as she was distracted by Erika's behavior. The bailiff began to speak while Nicole and Erika took their seats.

"On behalf of California, the city of San Francisco, Erika Johnson, you were ordered to appear in court for murder charges brought against you on September 25th, 2020, how do you plead?"

Erika continued shaking in her seat with her back hunched, unable to utter a word. Nicole then took over and stood up.

"Erika pleads not guilty, by reason of insanity your honor!"

Nicole noticed from the corner of her eye Erika slowly standing, then fainting to the ground. Nicole and the officers in the room tended to Erika, making sure that she was okay. Erika slightly came to and was helped back into her seat. Nicole then requested to speak to the judge in his chambers. She strongly believed that Erika wouldn't survive another night in jail due to her mental state. Both Nicole and Erika sat in the Judge's chambers, and Nicole asked that Erika be placed on house arrest so that she could be comfortable and protected while awaiting trial.

"House arrest? Yes, of course, Nicole. While we're at it, I can place her at the Fairmont Hotel, get a couple of guards to rotate shifts," The judge replied in sarcasm.

"Oh, I didn't think you'd go for it that easily, but yes, that would be perfect, thank you."

"No! Do you not hear my sarcasm? It would be perfect, but it's not going to happen. At best, we can make sure that she's treated if need be by a psychiatrist at the jail. But unfortunately, your friend is on trial for murder. You don't get rewarded with a vacation. You know that, Nicole."

Erika was tended to by the guard, and given a glass of water. At that moment, the guard began escorting Erika out of the room; Nicole followed and had a chance to whisper to Erika.

"Hang in there; everything is going to be okay."

"No, it's not, I did all that shit for nothing," Erika whispered back before she was escorted out of the room.

Nicole wasn't sure what to believe at that point. Was Erika really insane, or was she playing the game better than everyone else? Nicole was still very concerned for Erika, not knowing how she'd survive another night in jail. She made sure that Erika would be closely monitored and checked on by the psychiatrist on site. Later that evening, Nicole arrived home and was greeted by Ruth and Jeremiah. They eagerly waited up in the living room dressed in their pajamas for their mother to come home.

"Hi my darlings, I missed you. How was your day?" Nicole reached for a hug.

"I never got to show you my paper duck, look?" Ruth shouted with excitement from her tiny voice.

"Wow, you made that, all by yourself?"

"Uh huh."

"I love it, can you make one special, for me?"

"Here we go again," Jeremiah said with disappointment as he held his head down.

"Hey, why the long face?" Nicole asked.

"I didn't get to make anything cool like Ruth did, I just dissected a cow's eyeball, and no one thinks it's cool."

"That's not true. I think it's really cool. Do you know why?" Jeremiah shook his head, no.

"Because it means that you have what it takes to be a special doctor someday. Ruth makes beautiful art, but you, my little prince, might save lives." Jeremiah quickly cheered up and hugged his mother.

"Alright, now time to get ready for bed."

Nicole reached out her hands for Jeremiah and Ruth to follow. Once upstairs, Nicole helped them with brushing their teeth and washing their faces. Daniel walked in and started a conversation with

Nicole as he attempted to kiss her on the cheek. Nicole instantly jumped away, avoiding his touch.

"Hey, are you all right?" Daniel asked with concern.

"Yes, sorry, I just ...it's been a long couple of days."

"I know it must be a lot on you." Daniel attempted to rub Nicole's shoulders to offer her comfort, but she made it clear that she didn't want to be touched, at least not by him.

"Daniel please, I don't feel like being touched right now." Nicole continued helping the twins get ready for bed.

"Sorry! I won't touch you anymore."

"I'm sorry, I just need to figure out what I'm going to do. I don't know how I'm going to approach this court situation with Erika."

Nicole used work as an excuse when in actuality, she felt guilty about her infidelity.

The phone began to ring, and Daniel went to answer. Nicole finished helping the twins and began washing their faces. Daniel came back with the telephone, letting Nicole know that she had a call. Nicole was smart enough not to give her home number to the women she meets, so she had an instant idea of who might be on the other end. Daniel took over, getting the children ready for bed; Nicole answered the call and headed to the bedroom for privacy.

"Hi Veronica, I'm guessing you've seen the news?"

"Seen the news, I am the news. Did Erika convince you to enter that crazy ass insanity plea?"

"No, Veronica, she did not, it was my idea."

"Nicole, I know how much you love her and that you like to pretend you are big sister/mother to her, but this case could ruin you, what if you lose?"

"You don't think I've considered everything, the outcomes, the risk that I'm taking. Erika needs a lawyer."

"No, she needs a better therapist, and she needs to pay for what she did."

"How can you say that? She's our friend."

"Yes, our friend who has committed murder."

"She's mentally ill, Veronica."

"Oh my fucking God! She's not mentally ill; she is playing you. She might be insane, but she's 100 percent aware of her actions. Trust me!"

"Good night, Veronica!"

Nicole hung up the phone, slightly annoyed by Veronica's disapproval and negative opinions. Nicole didn't understand why Veronica was so quick to condemn Erika and her actions. Nicole didn't care whether Erika was mentally insane or not. She just wanted to make sure that Erika wouldn't spend her life in prison. Nicole went on with her night, tucking Ruth and Jeremiah into bed.

Erika was also preparing for bed as she sat down on a hard cot in a cold cell. Two other women shared the cell with her, chatting away. Erika didn't trust the women; she really didn't trust anyone and worried if the women would do something to her the second she closed her eyes. Erika then swung her legs on top of the cot and rested her body, placing her arms over her chest. Erika stared up at the ceiling feeling defeated and worried about her future. She then placed her hands in the openings of her sweater for warmth, and let out a sigh,

"Fuck, what the hell am I going to do now?"

2

Jasmine and Bobby

I'd like to go back to the beginning and tell you where their stories began, starting with Jasmine and Bobby. Almost two decades have passed since these two meet in high school, sophomore year. Bobby was the captain of the football team, and Jasmine was the school's science nerd. These two were complete opposites; never even spoke a word to one another until the end of sophomore year. They both shared the same homeroom, and would often run into each other during meal period. Jasmine was never the type to have, or need popularity to feel complete. Hence, she didn't have a lot of friends growing up. Jasmine was more of a loner, even ate lunch alone on most days. But that wasn't because she couldn't make friends, however, because she chose to focus her energy on her studies.

Jasmine felt as if most of the students around her weren't as mature as she was.

Jasmine also spent most of her time researching Earth, organisms, and mental health disorders. She became fascinated and almost obsessed with the different mental health conditions, as she had a cousin who was bipolar and schizophrenic. During Jasmine's lunch periods, she'd often sneak into the library, and stuff a few chicken nuggets into her pockets, as she'd eat and study at the same time. One particular day, Jasmine was in the library studying, and Bobby just happened to be in the library at the same time.

Bobby was a bit mischievous back then, and kind of still is to this day. He would bully other students and was also a bit of a player with the girls. With his mocha chocolate skin, muscular body, and a clean-shaven face, the girls quickly flocked to him. Bobby was the kind of person who never had to worry about having a date; there was always a girl waiting in line to be his arm piece. Bobby grew up in a semi-large family with two older brothers, a younger sister, and both of his parents.

So, when Bobby noticed Jasmine sitting at a computer with her round glasses resting perfectly on top of her nose, he approached. Bobby's intentions were not pure, as he intended to make a fool out of Jasmine. It was Bobby's thing. He got off on being a bully, and it fed his self-esteem. He enjoyed, even more, entertaining his friends in the process. Bobby saw Jasmine as a nerd that he could take advantage of and embarrass but was he surprised to find out that Jasmine was nobody's fool. Bobby's friends walked over with him, and they approached Jasmine.

"Hey there, what are you doing?" Bobby asked insincerely.

Jasmine turned around, stared at Bobby and his friends, and sarcastically replied,

"I'm minding my own business, which is something you should do." Bobby's friends got a chuckle out of Jasmine's reply. Bobby quickly became embarrassed and said,

"Bitch you better watch who you are talking

to, that's why you don't have any friends with your ugly ass. Looking like a damn scarecrow."

Jasmine was anything but ugly. She was attractive; had a thick shape, smooth cocoa brown skin, beautiful hazel eyes, and newly twisted dreads.

Bobby thought that by insulting her, he would not only embarrass Jasmine but also hide his real attraction. Although they never spoke until that day, Bobby always had a secrete crush but was too embarrassed to admit it. He also felt a girl like Jasmine would reject him, which she did.

"And you're an ignorant, uneducated, uncouth disgrace who probably can't multiply two by two. It's a shame that underneath all of that, there's nothing but cobwebs where your brain should be." Jasmine left Bobby and his two friends in shock as she stood up and fled from the computer table. Bobby then watched as Jasmine walked out of the room and instantly felt he needed to mend his bruised ego.

From that day forward, Bobby's mission was to get Jasmine to see a different side of him and win her over. Forget about a high school diploma; Bobby was trying to graduate with honors studying Jasmine Brown. However, Jasmine wasn't persuaded like the rest of the girls. Even though Bobby apologized for the comment that he made about her appearance, and for his actions, Jasmine didn't buy it. Bobby would make himself known to her by drawing attention or acting out in class. He even went to the extreme of being her secrete Santa and bought a 14k diamond bracelet. Bobby came from wealth, so for him, money grew on trees.

But it wasn't until one cold, wet, rainy fall morning, that Jasmine and Bobby were able to have a real conversation. The wind blew heavily as Jasmine stood outside, down the street from her house, waiting for the school bus to arrive. Jasmine stood at this particular stop every morning since freshman year. She held on tight to her umbrella, but suddenly, it turned itself inside out from the pressure of the wind. Jasmine was completely exposed to the storm and drenched from head to toe. Just as she started to scream, a bright red BMW pulled up in front of her.

Bobby ran out to offer her his umbrella and a ride to school. Jasmine wanted to refuse, but she knew she couldn't stand out there any longer in the pouring rain, so she took his offer. Though Jasmine was grateful, she was still very cautious of Bobby.

But slowly, Jasmine let her guard down. It helped that Bobby was handsome, but he made an effort to show Jasmine that his hollow interior was filled with heart and insecurity. They started dating six months later, and from that point on, they became an item.

After high school, Jasmine and Bobby got accepted into the City College of San Francisco criminal justice program. Bobby's father was a police officer, and he felt he needed to follow in his father's footsteps. Being that Jasmine and Bobby spent every moment of every day together, her goals meshed with his as they became one. They grew to think as one person, sharing the same interests and hobbies. Though it was nice having a partner in every sense of the word, they forgot to make time to explore themselves as individuals, thus becoming codependent on one another. Bobby didn't mind having his woman by his side; it soothed his insecurities and made him feel important. But, whenever Jasmine had the thought of doing things without Bobby, he quickly became possessive. Like a lot of dysfunctional relationships, Bobby had gotten used to the idea of having

Jasmine to himself. When she started to make friends, it quickly became a problem.

It all began the day Jasmine met Erika. Jasmine was taking a restroom break during one of her lectures and was immediately disturbed by the sounds of whimpering coming from the stall next to hers. The restroom was quite large with about ten stalls, and with just the two of them inside, the sound echoed from one end of the room to the other. Jasmine wasn't quite sure what to think of it and tried to exit the restroom making as little noise as possible. But the louder the sobbing became, Jasmine couldn't help but to pry.

"Are you okay?" Jasmine walked closer to the stall and stood with her ear close to the door.

"Yeah, I'm fine." The voice softly said back.

"Well I could hear you, sounds like you were crying, did something happen to you?"

There was immediate silence, and after waiting for a reply, Jasmine decided to mind her own business and stepped away. "Well, I hope you feel better." Jasmine started to walk out of the restroom but was stopped by the voice coming from the stall.

"My mom died. She was the only person I had left. I don't have anyone to talk to."

Jasmine immediately felt sympathy for the girl, and walked back toward her stall.

"Wow, I'm so sorry, what happened to her?" Jasmine's voice echoed as she pressed her face against the stall door.

"She had schizophrenia; she committed suicide."

"Damn, that's horrible. My cousin, he also died when he was young, he was bipolar and schizophrenic."

"What happened to him?"

"He was picked on a lot in school, teased about how he looked and talked. One day he was walking home from school, some asshole killed him. It was a hit and run. The police still never found the guy, or girl I guess, who did it." Jasmine slowly sat down on the floor with her back against the stall door.

"I'm sorry, that sucks, my mom was the only family I had left, I don't know what I'm going to do without her."

"It will be okay, it's going to hurt a lot for a while, but you will heal from this. Just know that one day, you will be reunited again. I'm sorry, I'm not the best at this kind of thing."

"It's okay; no one ever knows what to say. What's your name?"

"Jasmine, what's yours?"

"Erika."

"Nice to meet you, Erika, let me know if you ever want to blow off some steam. I like to jog in the mornings on the beach. It helps."

"Sure!" Erika then opened the stall door and caught Jasmine off guard as she was using the door to rest her back.

"Oh shit, I'm sorry," Erika said.

"No, you're good," Jasmine laughed and stood up. "Do you have your phone on you?"

"Yeah, why?" Erika pulled out her phone.

"Take my number, you shouldn't have to go through these times alone," Jasmine smiled and gave Erika her phone number. And from that day forward, the two of them became best friends.

Erika tried to fill the void in her life with Jasmine as she became her new person. In a way, Jasmine attached herself to Erika because she was the first real girl friend that she's had. But with Erika being a hopeless romantic, she allowed herself to have romantic feelings for Jasmine. Erika quickly became disappointed when she realized that Jasmine wasn't a fan of softball, but much preferred the all-male league.

One evening, Jasmine invited Erika over to her place to hang out, which she shared with Bobby. Jasmine and Bobby were together for about two years before they decided to get a place together. Of course, Erika met Bobby the few times she was invited over but always felt negative energy when Bobby came around. Erika secretly hated Bobby but kept her opinions to herself. She also sensed that Bobby was incredibly selfish and believed that Jasmine deserved better. So on this chilly fall evening, Erika came by dressed in a sweatshirt and pajama pants with a case of Oreo's in one hand and milk in the other. Jasmine was shocked by what Erika was wearing but was most surprised that she showed up with a gallon of milk.

"Girl, what's with the *Oreo* cookies and milk? This is not *The Parent Trap*. Jasmine laughed as she escorted Erika inside.

"Oreo's are my favorite comfort food. You can't go wrong with Oreo's."

"Alright, I guess I wouldn't mind a cookie or two."

Erika and Jasmine agreed to help each other with their studies, and it was also a way for them to keep in contact. They would often talk about science, conspiracy theories, and even the loved ones they've lost. While Jasmine was helping Erika with her math, she became curious asking herself, "Does she like me, should I try to kiss her?" Erika asked herself those questions while they sat on the floor. Jasmine leaned in to take a closer look at the book in Erika's lap. As soon as she looked back up, Erika's lips were touching hers. Jasmine immediately backed away, and Erika freaked out.

"I'm sorry I don't know why I did that." Erika gave the two of them some distance.

"No, you're fine. But I'm not gay, and you know that I have a boyfriend, right?"

"Bobby, I know." Erika said in disappointment.

"Yes Bobby! I'm 100 percent straight, and I don't judge you or anything. I just hope we can still be friends?"

"Yes, I shouldn't have done that, I'm sorry."

"It's okay! Just as long as we are on the same page." Jasmine smiled and reassured Erika that everything was okay. That's what Erika always loved about Jasmine, how she never seemed to have a judgmental bone in her body, at least when it came to their friendship. And even though Jasmine knew Erika might have feelings for her, it didn't change her opinions of her. Jasmine knew, to a certain degree, how lonely Erika was and didn't have any intentions to disappear from her life. Although Erika was slightly embarrassed, she realized that having Jasmine's friendship would be better than not having her at all. While they continued studying and enjoying Oreo's, they were soon interrupted when Bobby came home.

Bobby seemed to have had a bad day, and rushed inside to speak to Jasmine, but was caught off guard when he noticed Erika.

"You again, damn! Don't you have a place of your own to go to?" Bobby rudely asked as he stared at the two of them, sitting on the floor next to an open container of cookies and milk.

"Excuse you? Don't be so rude! I don't treat your friends like when you have them over, say hello!"

Bobby ignored Jasmine as he continued to glare sternly. Bobby's thoughts took him away as he became jealous. Bobby knew to a certain degree that Erika was not only gay but that she fancied Jasmine. Bobby then decided to greet Erika, but not in a pleasant way.

"Hi, and goodbye! I need to talk to my girlfriend in privacy."

"Bobby!" Jasmine shouted, irate by his rudeness.

"It's okay, I should go anyway, I will catch you tomorrow." Erika got up quickly and grabbed her things, but left the cookies and milk.

"I'm sorry, Erika, I will call you. Don't forget your cookies and milk." Jasmine went to reach for the cookies, and Erika suggested that she keep them. Erika smiled and went on about her day, leaving Jasmine to deal with Bobby's ignorance. Bobby stood there with his hands on his hips while he judged her.

"You two sure have been spending a lot of time together lately." Jasmine quickly became defensive and troubled by Bobby's jealousy.

"She's my friend, am I not allowed to have friends?"

"No, that's not what I said, that's not what I'm saying. You're just never around anymore when I need you."

"What? We live together! I come home every

single night to you! I'm always around. You need to grow up and stop acting like a spoiled little boy. What you did was childish."

That was it. The moment Bobby felt the dagger to his ego. Bobby wasn't the kind of guy who liked to be seen as anything less than a man. Bobby already struggled with codependency and attachment issues, and Jasmine's comment was the icing on the cake.

"What the fuck did you just say, I'm a little boy?" Bobby stepped closer.

"Yes, you're acting like a jealous little boy, grow up." Bobby's blood boiled while he stood in front of her, contemplating whether he should smack her. Before he knew it, his hand flew across Jasmine's face releasing a loud SMACK.

Jasmine was surprised as she cupped her face in her hand. Jasmine was never the kind of person to let someone make a fool of her, so she slapped him back. Things quickly escalated between them as they both became physical with one another. Bobby pushed Jasmine, and she lost her balance falling to the ground. Jasmine then quickly got up and kicked Bobby in the groin.

"What the fuck is wrong with you? You hit

women now?" Bobby held his groin as he endured the pain and slowly fell to the floor. Jasmine walked closer and stood in front of him, ready to strike again. All Bobby could do was sit there in pain, staring up at Jasmine with a cringed face.

"Don't you ever put your hands on me again," Jasmine said sternly.

"I'm sorry I shouldn't have done that. But you didn't need to kick me in my dick."

"I'm not going to be in an abusive relationship. We're not even married, we don't have kids, I don't have to put up with this shit, and I won't." Jasmine began to walk out of the living room, but Bobby cried out,

"Wait, Jasmine?"

Jasmine continued to walk out of the living room, and Bobby slowly got up to chase after her. They both hurried into the bedroom, and Bobby pleaded,

"Jasmine, please, I promise it will never happen again. Just don't leave me." Jasmine froze, taking a minute to hear Bobby out.

Jasmine knew in the back of her mind that she should leave, but continued to stay. And a few months later, she found herself accepting his proposal and becoming his wife. Jasmine has mentally and emotionally dug a hole that's gotten too deep for her to climb out of. It's just a matter of her doing the mental work and finally finding the courage to leave. Jasmine wanted to believe that things would change, that he would never hit her again, but the more she forgave him, the less guilty he began to feel for his actions. Jasmine would soon realize that marrying Bobby would be the biggest mistake of her life.

Jasmine consulted with a lawyer five years after she and Bobby married, and that's when she met Nicole. Jasmine wanted to know how she could rid herself of the marriage in which she trapped herself. Her marriage began to cost her not only her life but also the friendship she built with Erika. Bobby's jealousy and abuse kept her from spending as much time as she used to with Erika. At times, Jasmine would have to sneak out for social gatherings, because she knew once Bobby became jealous, that it would lead to another physical fight. Although Jasmine wanted to leave, she always found herself going back to him, no matter how bad things had gotten. It wasn't until recently, after 15 years of being together, when Jasmine realized that she needed to get out.

3

Nicole and Robyn

Nicole was at home, working on Erika's case. It was mid-morning, and she had the whole house to herself. Nicole prepared in the living room on the sofa with her files and got ready to relax with a cup of coffee until she got a knock at the door. Nicole placed her cup on the table in front of her and walked over towards the door. She was surprised to see Jasmine standing on the other side.

"Hey, I'm surprised to see you here, aren't you supposed to be chasing crime or something?"

"No, I took the day off, Bobby and I got into

another fight." Jasmine invited herself inside, and Nicole followed behind, watching as Jasmine took a seat on the couch.

"Well come on in, can I get you a cup of coffee too?" Nicole said sarcastically.

"Yes, please, black." Nicole chuckled to herself as she went into the kitchen to pour Jasmine a hot cup of coffee. Jasmine then made herself comfortable on the couch and waited for Nicole to return. Once Nicole returned with a steaming hot mug of coffee, she sat next to Jasmine, and began to question,

"What the hell happened this time?"

"What do you mean, this time?" Jasmine said in defense.

"Honey, I don't know why you're even still with that man."

"It's not easy like you think it is, just to leave."

"You should have left him the day you came to my office asking for legal advice, do you remember what I told you?"

"Yes, you said that doing what's hard just might be what saves my life."

"Look at what happened to Erika; she was a ticking time bomb waiting to explode, don't let that be you too. I can't lose both of my best friends," Nicole said with concern.

"Can we not talk about that right now, I need to take my mind off everything. Let's talk about Erika, what's going on with her case, do you believe you can help her?"

"Honestly, I don't know. I found something in Erika's records from her therapy sessions, and I'm concerned that the prosecution will try to use it against us."

"What did you find?"

"A lot! It made me wonder, how well do we know each other, I mean, really?"

"Damn, what did you find out?" Jasmine sat close with her cup in her hand.

"Enough! Unfortunately, I can't share details about the case; you know that. I need to visit her, see if I can sort through this mess."

"Nicole, you're starting to scare me."

"Yeah, well, I'm scared for Erika. It's crazy to think that we've been friends for a decade, and I knew so little about her. I'm starting to wonder how well do you and I know each other…"

"I don't know, girl. I know that you're the only

one of us that seems to have it all together. You have this perfect life, family, career."

"Well, I don't have love."

"What do you mean, Daniel is obsessed over you. He adores you."

"Yes well, I wish I could return the feeling, but I can't. Life isn't always what it appears to be." Jasmine became confused by Nicole's reply because she's always believed that Nicole had a perfect marriage.

"I know that you've mentioned your attraction to women, do you think that's partly clouding your judgment?"

"Yes and No. I've come to realize that I am, in fact, 99.9 percent gay. I've known for quite a while now. I'm just so damn tired of lying to myself and pushing my true feelings under the rug." Nicole valued Jasmine's opinions, and knowing that she is heterosexual, Nicole never felt comfortable enough to open up about her sexuality completely.

"I've had flings here and there, but no matter how hard I try to replace her, I can't."

"Replace who?" Jasmine became even more confused.

"My first love. Before I married Daniel, I was

with a woman. I was too ashamed to be with her, to be out with her. She was beautiful, funny, intelligent, and always smelled of roses and cinnamon," Nicole smiled as she reflected on her past.

"Wow! H-how did I not know any of this?"

"Because I valued our friendship, I still value our friendship, and maybe I wanted that more than to unload my problems on you." Jasmine quickly sat up and put down her cup of coffee.

"Nicole, is that what you think, that I would judge you or be less of a friend?"

"I lost the one person in this world that I've ever truly loved because I was too ashamed to love her. Of course, I hid that part of myself from you. But now I'm starting to realize that I can't hide forever." Jasmine placed her hand gently over Nicole's.

"I love you, all of you, you are my best friend. I want you to be as free as you can be, and don't ever feel like you have to hide any parts of yourself from me." At that moment, Nicole felt relieved that finally, someone understood her, and they embraced one another.

"So, what was her name?" Jasmine quietly asked.

"Robyn, her name was Robyn."

"But Daniel, does he know any of this?" Jasmine asked while taking another sip of her coffee.

"No, he doesn't, and it's all a mess because I feel so guilty, especially when he tries to touch me, I completely flip out. Mind you, I have told him numerous times that I think we should take a break. I've even told him that I'm attracted to women. He just acts as if we've never had these conversations." Jasmine laughed at Nicole, who was trying to be serious.

"Seriously, the next day, he calls me, honey, and kisses me on the cheek."

"You do realize that it's because you let him? Of course, he's going to play the denial card, as long as you keep giving him hope." Nicole became confused as she stared back at Jasmine.

"What do you mean, giving him hope? I told him that I wanted to see other people."

"And yet, you're still here! Sleeping in the same bed, too, I'm guessing?" Nicole took a moment to think about what Jasmine said. Nicole never considered why Daniel didn't take her seriously because she hadn't taken herself seriously. Though Nicole claimed that she wanted to date other people, she continued to stay with Daniel.

"I'm going to visit Erika; you're welcome to stay here while I'm gone."

"I see you're still good at changing the subject." Nicole then got up from the sofa and began to walk out of the living room, leaving Jasmine feeling baffled as she chuckled to herself.

Later that evening, Nicole went to visit Erika at the county jail. Erika appeared even more distressed than she did the previous day. Her hair was a mess and barely clung to the ponytail it was attached to. It was clear to Nicole that Erika was not doing well as she approached with a smile. But as Erika sat there patiently waiting at the table, she could tell that underneath Nicole's smile was disappointment. Erika tried to ignore the negative thoughts that began to form in her mind. Erika smiled back as Nicole sat down in front of her.

"Hey, how are you?" Erika said, barely catching her breath.

"I'm doing okay, just worried about you. How are you holding up in here?"

"I'm hanging in there, trying to at least. I need you to get me out of here, Nicole."

"Listen, Erika; I've been working on your case,

I don't think I'm going to be able to get you out, at least not any time soon."

"You don't think you can get me out? San Francisco's best, can't fucking get me out?" Erika shouted in frustration.

"Calm down and lower your voice. I've been going through your files from your therapy sessions, and there are things in it that the prosecution will use against you."

"So wait a minute, they have my records from my therapy sessions? I thought those were supposed to be confidential?"

"Yes Erika, to an extent, but not in this case," Nicole paused before continuing, "What happened in Muir Woods? Do you remember?" Erika immediately remembered what Nicole was referring too, but tried to ignore her question.

"Erika, I cannot help you if you are not honest with me. I already know what's in these files, I just need you to tell me the truth about what happened." Erika sat there with her arms folded and began to feel judged.

"Do you know what I'm talking about Erika?"

"Yeah I remember."

"Was this the first time something like this happened, or the second?"

"You know, you have a lot of nerve sitting across from me judging me. Does Daniel know that you've been having affairs with other women since the day you got married? I wonder what he would say or do if he knew. I haven't used my phone time yet today, maybe I'll go find out for the both of us."

"Are you fucking kidding me? You're way out of line. Remember, my life isn't on trial!"

"Calm the fuck down." Erika sinisterly replied.

"Don't tell me to fucking calm down, I'm trying to save your life, and you're in here threatening me. I didn't tell you to choke your girlfriend to death!"

The room became quiet as Erika took offense to Nicole's remarks. In return, Nicole felt that Erika didn't appreciate the time she had been putting into trying to help her. Nicole took a moment to gather her thoughts and got her feelings in check before she spoke further.

"There is new evidence connecting you to a murder that happened five years ago. If you cannot tell me everything that happened that day, if you cannot be honest with me, there won't be a damn thing I can do to help you. I love you, but if you threaten me again, you won't only lose the best damn lawyer in this state, but you'll lose a best friend too. Now...I am going to ask you one more time, is there anything in these files that we need to discuss?" Erika took a moment to consider what Nicole asked before taking a deep breath and replying with,

"Yeah, there is, but I'm finished talking for today."

Nicole became afraid for Erika, fearful that if it were true that she committed another murder, it would be hard to convince a jury to not only feel sorry for her but to believe that she was insane. Erika asked to be taken back to her cell, leaving Nicole sitting alone. Later that evening, when Nicole was home in bed, she reflected on her visit with Erika. After being spooked, Nicole knew that if anyone were going to tell Daniel about her infidelities, she would tell him herself. Nicole and Daniel were chatting in bed, and she worked up the nerve once more to tell him her true feelings and asked,

"Daniel, can we talk?"

"Yeah, what's on your mind?" Daniel put down

the book he was reading and gave Nicole his attention.

"First, I want to say that I'm sorry I've been so distant. Lately, I've been trying to tell you how I feel, but you don't take it seriously, and honestly, maybe I haven't either."

"Is this about you wanting to date other...women?"

"No, well, yes, sort of. Daniel, I've realized over the years that I've not been honest with myself. I tried to push away my feelings, bury them deep, I just can't do it any longer." Daniel stared as if he was confused, and Nicole blurted out,

"Daniel, I am gay!" Daniel continued to stare at Nicole, who was desperately waiting for a response. Then out of the blue, Daniel began chuckling, turning red in the face. Nicole was instantly annoyed by Daniel's laughter as she tried her best to be serious.

"Oh honey, I love you... I'm going to bed." Daniel kissed Nicole on the cheek as he did every night, turned over, and went to sleep, leaving Nicole staring at the wall ahead.

Nicole became disappointed all over again; she hoped that maybe this time, Daniel would take her seriously. But there was a part of her that wasn't ready to push the subject further, so she slowly rested her head on her pillow. Nicole would lay awake, thinking about the past, and wondered if she would ever be free to truly be herself. Nicole partly felt as if she needed Daniel's approval to move on, and without that, Nicole felt stuck.

Nicole closed her eyes, and her thoughts took her to older memories, a time when she was in Law School after she and Daniel split during their senior year of high school. Nicole remembered a similar conversation she had with him on graduation day. Nicole was more of a free spirit back then and wasn't afraid to ask for space to explore herself, to be single.

During the five years Nicole was in college, she hadn't spoken to Daniel. Instead, she satisfied her cravings in her Legal Research class at USF School of Law. Nicole always stood out from the rest of her class, not only because of her smarts, but her looks as well. Nicole was always one to keep herself nice and polished. She wore the best skirts, power suits, and always kept her hair moisturized. Being one of the few women of color studying law, she felt very proud.

Though Nicole never missed a beat in class, she'd often get caught in a gaze staring at one of the other students. One student, in particular, was Robyn Reed. Nicole never had the opportunity to explore her sexuality. Coming from a homophobic family, Nicole never paid much mind to her occasional crushes. Not until one particular day in her Legal Research class, she finally worked up the nerve to speak to Robyn. It was just moments before the end of class. Robyn was sitting alone at a table near the front, and Nicole walked over with her books as she said to herself,

"Okay Nicole, you got this, just say hello."

Nicole placed her books gently on the table where Robyn was sitting and sat down next to her.

"Hi, I'm Nicole," She reached out her hand as she introduced herself.

"Oh hi, I'm Robyn, Robyn Reed." Robyn then shook Nicole's hand.

One interesting thing about Nicole is that she is very intuitive, and could always tell when someone was interested. The only battle Nicole seemed to struggle with was short talk.

"So, are you understanding this class? It's pretty tough, huh?" Nicole asked nervously.

"The class is pretty interesting, most definitely difficult. I don't really like writing long essays," Robyn smiled nervously and chuckled.

"Well, if you ever need any help, here's my number, writing is one of my many strong suits," Nicole smiled as she handed Robyn her phone number, which she already wrote down on a piece of paper. Nicole always had a little bit of a game; she wasn't afraid of rejection, mostly because it rarely happened. It was her first time, however, approaching another woman.

"Okay, I'll give you a call if I need anything." Robyn replied as she smiled and bit her bottom lip.

"I'll be waiting for your call."

The class was released, and Nicole got up from the table, leaving Robyn feeling bashful. It was no surprise to Nicole when she received a call later that evening. Nicole took it upon herself to invite Robyn over for a study date. Nicole made grilled chicken, mashed potatoes (which was her specialty), and spinach. Nicole was very confident in her cooking skills; in fact, there wasn't much of anything that Nicole didn't succeed at.

When Robyn arrived, Nicole greeted her at the

door, took her jacket, and politely asked Robyn to take off her shoes. Nicole then took her belongings and placed them in the closet. Another thing about Nicole, she is a total neat freak; everything has its place. Robyn was surprised when she walked inside and smelled the strong aroma of seasoned chicken.

"It smells so good in here, did you cook?"

"Yes, I made something for us to have while studying. There's also wine if you like?" Nicole asked as she directed Robyn into the dining room. The table was set, the light in the room was dim, and Nicole also lit a couple of candles.

"Wow, do you go all out like this for all of your study dates?" Robyn smiled.

"I'm sorry, is it too much?"

"No, no, not at all. I've honestly never had anyone make me a candlelight dinner before."

Nicole and Robyn took their seats at the dining room table, which was the perfect size for them to have enough space to eat and be close enough to talk. Nicole was always the kind of person who went after what she wanted, and she never gave anything less than 100 percent. Most people might say that Nicole was moving a little too fast, but

Nicole and Robyn both believed that life was too short to wait around for time to tell them how they felt. They both began to eat, and Robyn was amazed at how delicious the food was.

"Oh my God, this is amazing, you've got to give me your recipe," Robyn said and continued to indulge.

"I'm glad you like it. I was a little nervous," Nicole smiled.

"You, nervous? I don't think so. I've noticed you in class. I was honestly shocked when you gave me your number. I figured a woman like you would be..."

"Straight?" Nicole asked.

"Well, yeah. I'm sorry it's just that most females who are gay don't look like...you."

"And how do I look?" Nicole asked and then took a bite of her chicken.

"You're gorgeous, first of all. You seem much more mature for your age, and there's something different about you. You're classy, a bit controlling, and all the guys want to fuck you."

"Wow, controlling? It seems you have been paying attention, but not close enough. Otherwise, you would have noticed that I haven't given a fuck about any, *guys*. Excuse my French."

"Is that right?" Robyn raised her eyebrow.

"I've had my eye on you since the first day of class. You intrigued me," Nicole then took a sip of her wine.

"How so?" Robyn then mimicked Nicole by taking a sip of her wine as well.

"Your eyes when I first saw them I was instantly drawn to you. Some days they look grey, and other times, they look like a hazel brown. But the roundness of them pulled me in. It's like I could see inside your soul. Your hair, so curly and long, always smells of roses when I walk past you. The way you carry yourself, your clothes are always pressed just a little too hard, but I like that you take pride in your appearance. Your hands, so small, when you write, you always stick out your tongue like you're solving the world's biggest mystery. And your mind, you always ask questions that even I hadn't thought of. I could tell that you'd be someone I'd never get bored of, shall I go on?"

"Wow, that's no, that's..."

Nicole had amazed Robyn with the observations she made. They both sat close to one another.

Nicole felt Robyn's energy, and that energy transferred to her. Nicole put down her fork and calmly reached over towards Robyn for a kiss. But before Nicole and Robyn touched lips, Nicole took a moment to gaze into Robyn's eyes, and she then kissed her passionately. At that moment, everything felt right, and Nicole felt chills that ran from the top of her head, down to her thighs.

For a brief moment, Nicole was vulnerable, not knowing what to say or do. Nicole didn't expect to feel so connected to Robyn; how the touch of Robyn's hand against her face gave her butterflies. Nicole instantly felt she was right where she needed to be. Robyn then began to unbutton her blouse while Nicole watched like a school kid. Although Nicole was confident, fearless, and even intimidating, she never had sex with a woman. Nicole has only ever had sex with Daniel at that point.

So as Robyn continued to remove her pink-laced bra, Nicole stopped her, stood up, and grabbed Robyn by the hand to lead her to her bedroom.

"Follow me,"

Nicole confidently said. Robyn then stood up and followed Nicole to her bedroom. As Nicole walked Robyn into her room, they both stopped at the foot of the bed. The room was dimly lit, allowing the two of them to see just enough of each other. Nicole pulled Robyn close by placing her hand on the small of her back, and she began kissing her gently on the neck. Robyn responded as she quietly moaned, and Nicole then softly kissed Robyn on the lips while removing her bra.

Robyn's breasts were perky and perfectly round. Nicole began kissing Robyn from her neck down to her nipples, and she sucked ever so gently. Nicole then sat Robyn on her bed and proceeded to take off her own shirt and bra. Nicole laid Robyn down as she continued kissing her.

"You seem to know what you're doing, have you been with a woman before?" Robyn asked, as she would lay there exposed and vulnerable.

"No, I haven't. Is this too much, should I stop?"

"No, I want to keep going, but let me show you what I like." Robyn smiled and switched positions with Nicole. Robyn was now on top of Nicole, straddled over her pelvis, and began kissing her. Breast against breast nipple against nipple, they began to make love for the first time. Though they hadn't spoken until that day, they both felt as if they'd known each other for years, and for the first time in Nicole's life, she felt complete. Nicole held Robyn in her arms after their passionate night of lovemaking, and they engaged in pillow talk.

"Do you think we knew each other in a different life?" Robyn asked quietly.

"I think anything is possible. I've never felt this way with anyone, instantly connected. I've never been so intrigued by anyone as much as I have been with you." Nicole smiled and kissed Robyn on the forehead.

"I think that before we're born, we are balls of energy floating around, traveling between realms, but we travel as one with our soul mates. That's how I felt with you. As if everything I had been lacking, it was instantly filled the moment we connected. Maybe that's the test. Once separated on earth, having enough faith to find each other again, and move forward as one." Robyn's thoughts carried away as she rested her head on Nicole's bosom.

"You sound like someone I know." Nicole smiled. "Who?"

"I'm sorry, he's my ex, Daniel. He's always

talking about outer space and theories, but I like your theory."

"What happened to you and this, Daniel?"

"He's no one to worry about; I shouldn't have brought him up, I'm sorry."

"Don't be sorry. I want to learn everything there is to know about you." Robyn turned to her side and looked Nicole in the eye.

"Daniel and I were best friends growing up. I didn't have many female friends; I always hung out with the boys. Daniel was, he was special. He was always kind, and of course, as we got older, we thought that we should be together, but it never felt right to me, like this, with you. If you're wondering if you have anything to worry about, you don't. I'm exactly where I want to be."

From that moment on, Nicole and Robyn became inseparable. They inspired each other, challenged each other, loved, and trusted one another as their relationship grew. Everything was perfect until it wasn't.

A year later, into their relationship, it was the holiday season, and Robyn wanted to celebrate Christmas together. Robyn was eager to meet Nicole's family, and she wanted Nicole to meet hers. Although Nicole adored Robyn, she wasn't quite ready to come out to her family. Remember, this was back in the early 2000s, not too far from the 90s, and being gay was still very taboo. Nicole didn't mind meeting Robyn's family, but it quickly became an issue when Nicole didn't want to introduce Robyn to hers. Robyn and Nicole sat on the couch in the living room of Nicole's apartment. It was late in the afternoon, and they both were arguing about where to have Christmas dinner.

"I don't understand, it's been a year, and I haven't met anyone in your family. Are you embarrassed to be seen with me?" Robyn asked.

"Of course, I'm not embarrassed by you. I've told you how my family is. They wouldn't accept you like your family is willing to accept me. It would be a horrible Christmas if we went to my parent's house."

"So, when do you plan on telling your parents about us, or do you plan to at all?"

"Yes, I will eventually, just not today!"

Robyn didn't understand why Nicole didn't have the courage to be honest about her sexuality, as she did with other things. Robyn's patience grew thin the longer she waited.

"I can't live like this forever. I want to hold your hand in public and be introduced as your girlfriend, your partner, not your friend."

"I can't do that right now, can't you understand?" Nicole shouted from frustration.

"Yeah, I understand."

"Thank You!" Nicole took a deep breath and tried to reach for Robyn's hand, but Robyn instantly rejected it.

"I understand that you can't do that right now, but I also can't do this right now either. I've always been the one to give up my needs, who goes with the flow, but I won't keep doing that. There are things that I need as well, and whenever you're ready to accept yourself, for who you are, give me a call."

Robyn got up and stormed out of the apartment, leaving Nicole sitting alone on the couch. Nicole thought to go after Robyn but knew that she wouldn't be able to give Robyn what she needed, and so, Nicole let her go. That was a heartbreaking day for Nicole, watching the love of her life walk out of her life on Christmas day. Nicole began to doubt herself. She felt as though she'd never be comfortable with herself as a gay woman, a black gay woman, in fact. Her family didn't accept it, and in a way, Nicole didn't accept it either. Nicole decided that if she couldn't be with the one person she loved, she'd never give her heart to anyone else again.

Later that night, after feeling lonely, brokenhearted, and spending Christmas day alone in tears, she gave Daniel a call. Nicole knew that she could always count on Daniel's friendship, and that was what she needed at the moment. Nicole didn't have the same feelings for him as she did for Robyn, but she also didn't want to be alone. Daniel was eager to be apart of her life again, even if deep down, he knew Nicole would never love him the way he loved her.

In a way, Nicole went back to Daniel as a way of punishing herself, punishing herself for not having the courage to be who she truly is. Nicole once again pushed her feelings away and buried them deep. As the years went by, she and Daniel married and had the twins. Nicole got used to lying to herself so much that she almost forgot how it felt to truly be in love. As Nicole would lay awake in bed next to Daniel, remembering her past 15 years ago, she decided that she no longer wanted to live a lie. Nicole immediately sat up, pulled the covers back, and stood up to put on her house shoes. Nicole grabbed her cell phone from the nightstand, walked into the bathroom, and dialed a number. Nicole waited with anticipation to hear a familiar voice on the other end say,

"Hello?" Robyn answered softly. Nicole almost wept, but she held back her tears and smiled.

4

Veronica and Gloria

Later in the week, Veronica was scrambling around her room as she did every morning at 3 am, to get ready for work. Veronica and Gloria live in a beautiful but older home, and the floors tend to squeak in places. Though at this point, they each know where not to walk to cause the least noise. This has been Veronica's routine every day, Monday through Friday, for the past two years. Veronica respected Gloria by tiptoeing out of bed, as she tried her best not to make a sound.

Veronica would go downstairs, brew a nice fresh pot of coffee, and indulge herself before taking a shower. Veronica loved how the soap lathered against her skin and scalp, and would often spend longer in the shower than she should. After Veronica finished her shower, she would spend another 30 minutes going through her closet, trying to find the best dress to wear for the day. After finally choosing a dress that she liked, she'd pick out a pair of heels to go with it. Veronica was the kind of woman who took pride in her looks and had more shoes and clothes in her closet than the room for them to fit. Every morning, before Veronica would leave for work, she'd pause at the door, standing there, taking a moment to admire the love of her life. However, this morning, Veronica walked towards Gloria and got caught in a gaze that took her to another time.

Ten years ago, when Veronica was 19 years old, she finally worked up the courage to transfer to the University of California, Berkeley. Veronica was always passionate about drama, performing, or anything artistic, and thrived off of the attention. So it was natural that she took an interest in Journalism. Coming from a small town in Texas, Veronica was ready to live the big city life, but little did she know what big city living would truly mean. Not only would rent be three times more expensive than it was back home, but people always seemed to be in a rush. One bright fall morning, Veronica eagerly waited at a bus stop in Oakland, which would transfer her to Berkeley, to arrive for her first day of college.

Over the years, the number of homeless people living on the streets increased, and they were always walking by asking for change at this particular station. There were a couple of other people waiting at the stop as well, but Veronica didn't pay any mind to the people around, not until she was approached by one of the homeless men standing nearby.

"Excuse me, do you have some change to spare?"

"No, I don't," Veronica rudely said as she walked to a different part of the stop.

Walking to another area, however, didn't stop people from coming up to her. Veronica was always quite the dresser, as she stood there wearing a silky white blouse, brown sued skirt, and heels to match. Veronica's first mistake was waving how much money she had in front of the homeless by dressing as if she was Queen Elizabeth's niece.

Before Veronica could even think about taking a seat, someone else approached her.

"Excuse me, sexy mama, do you have any change to spare so I can get something to eat?"

Veronica's eyes grew gigantic from the annoyance she began to feel.

"No, I do not! Please, why don't you ask those people over there?" Veronica pointed to a group of people who were also waiting for the bus.

"I'm not asking them, I'm asking you."

"Oh my God!" Veronica stormed off back to the other end of the stop, and as she stood there, a woman approached from behind, who chuckled at the situation.

"You shouldn't have worn that." The voice said from behind; Veronica quickly turned around and shouted,

"What?"

"I'm sorry, but as long as you look like, that, people will assume you have a lot of money."

Veronica looked at the woman wearing a windbreaker jacket and black slacks. Veronica was confused by the woman's statement as she looked down at her outfit, then back up at the woman.

"What do you mean, what's wrong with what I'm wearing?"

"How much did that outfit cost?"

"I don't know, two, maybe 300 after the shoes. I love these heels, aren't they cute?"

"I guess, but I'm just trying to figure out how you can afford a 300 dollar outfit, but you can't spare five bucks?"

"What!" Veronica became aggravated, and the same homeless man who approached her not even five minutes ago walked by again. He lingered around, waiting for another opportunity. The woman noticed, turned toward him, and reached into her pocket as she continued speaking to Veronica.

"Relax, I'm just giving you a hard time." The woman laughed as she handed the man a five-dollar bill.

"If you don't want them to approach you, keep your head down, and don't wear that outfit ever again or anything like it."

The woman smiled and began to walk toward the bench as the bus arrived.

"Yeah, I'll keep that in mind. Um, who are you? I didn't catch your name?"

"I'm Nicole, and you are?"

"Veronica."

"Okay Veronica, nice to meet you." Nicole stepped onto the bus and went on about her day. Veronica got on after her and didn't think anything else of the interaction. She was just thrilled to be away from that stop.

When Veronica finally arrived at the University of California, Berkeley, she left all that worry and frustration behind. Immediately, Veronica was like a kid again, excited, and eager to start the first day of college in a big city. Veronica was studying Journalism, but also had a knack for photography. She was fascinated with the art of creation, so she majored in Journalism and minored in photography. Veronica tried to make friends her first day in class, but it wasn't as easy as she expected. Being an outsider from a different state, and also having a slight accent, people mostly thought she was interesting but didn't take the time to get to know her.

Veronica quickly learned that in California, most people were focused on themselves. Everyone had something that they were trying to accomplish. Though Veronica was trying to achieve dreams of her own, she still wanted to make California feel like home. Later that day, after her classes were over, Veronica headed back home. Although she was excited to be a student at a highly accredited college, she still felt something was missing from her life. Veronica kept her hopes up that she would make friends as she headed back home to Oakland, and waited at the bus stop. The ride going back into Oakland was peaceful, as she had time to listen to her music, and dream of what tomorrow might bring. It wasn't until Veronica waited at the same stop where she stood earlier that morning, that she began to worry.

"Hey ma, how you doin?" A man approached Veronica from behind, dressed in baggy sweats and a shirt that looked as if it had been worn for days.

"Uh, fine, thanks."

As the man continued walking closer, Veronica tried to keep her distance and slowly backed away.

"So whatcha got there?"

"What do you mean?"

"I want what you got in that purse."

"I'm not giving you my fucking purse, back off."

Veronica clenched tightly to her purse, and the

man continued approaching until Veronica was backed up into a corner.

"You don't have to give it to me, because I'm going to take it."

As soon as he said the words, take it, he snatched the purse out of her hands and ran for the hills. Veronica ran after him as fast as she could, but her sued heels just weren't cut out for the job. Veronica worried she would lose all of her money, including her credit cards. As the man got away, and the residents of the neighborhood stopped and stared, Veronica, kneeled to the ground in the middle of the sidewalk, and cried out.

Veronica didn't understand why someone would do such a thing. Coming from a sheltered life in a small town in Jefferson, TX, Veronica was not correctly prepared for the horrors of big city living. So as she sat there feeling embarrassed and terrified, she could only think of one release,

"Fuck!"

Veronica screamed, and once she finished, she slowly stood up. Veronica knew that she would need to figure something out and fast. She began to walk down the streets asking around for the nearest Police station, because not only did the robber steal her purse, but her phone inside it also. A couple of hours later, and nearly out of breath, Veronica found a police station.

"Finally, Jesus Christ."

Veronica slowly walked inside with sweat dripping from her face, and her clothes a mess. Her 300-dollar outfit was ruined, but she didn't care at the point, she just needed to get her purse back. Veronica then noticed a woman at the front desk and approached her.

"I need to make a report. Someone attacked me and stole my purse. It had all of my credit cards, money, and my phone inside of it. I don't know what to do."

"Okay, calm down. Just have a seat, and I'll get an officer to speak with you."

Veronica slowly walked over to the waiting area but was skeptical that there would be anything they could do to help, especially since it had already been hours since her purse was stolen. An officer soon approached Veronica and took her inside, where she could make her report. This Officer was a young woman, friendly, and excited to possibly have a case. Veronica could scan her body language, and could also tell that she was probably new while gazing at her name tag, which read, Smith. The two sat down at a desk, and Officer Smith began to ask questions.

"Can I get you anything to drink, water?"

"No, I just want my fucking purse back." Veronica looked up at Officer Smith, who was staring back at her and Veronica went on to say, "Well actually, I could use some water, thanks."

The Officer went back to get Veronica a bottle of water. While Veronica sat alone, waiting for Officer Smith to return, she became curious, taking a look around at her desk. Veronica noticed certificates, photos, even a wedding photo that the Officer proudly displayed. When Officer Smith returned with the bottle of water, Veronica gulped it down so fast that she could hardly catch her breath. The Officer stared at her with concern and began to question her again.

"So, tell me ma'am, what happened?"

"I was attacked, I was waiting for the bus down by Martin Luther king something Blvd, I don't know, I'm not from here. This man wearing old clothes, baggy sweat pants, and a dingy black shirt, attacked me and took my purse."

"When you say attack, did he physically harm you?"

"Yes, by stealing my purse, and now I don't have any money."

"No, I mean, did he touch you?"

"Will that make you search for my purse faster if I say yes?" Veronica said with sarcasm.

"I just need to gather all of the facts; this way, it will help us identify this person better. Often, the same thieves you see out in the streets have been arrested before; we may have records of him in the system. They also often display repeated behaviors, so that's why I'd like to know, did he physically harm you?"

"Well no, he just threatened me, stole my purse, and ran. You know, I thought this would be a great experience, moving out here, but it has turned out to be one of my worst decisions."

"No, it's just a terrible day, and you just have to learn how to move out here," Officer Smith tried to comfort Veronica.

"Listen, are you going to help me, I mean, are you capable, because you seem new no offense. I already don't have any family or friends out here, I'm alone, and I can't even buy myself a meal tonight. I'm starting to understand what these homeless people go through. Oh, my God! Am I being punished for not giving that homeless man any money?"

"No! Listen, I'm going to do everything that I can to help you. Let's finish this report. Can you describe what this man looked like?"

Veronica continued to file her report as she described the man's appearance. Veronica was instructed to close any card accounts that she may have had in her wallet. Without having a phone, Veronica wasn't sure how to do this, so the Officer allowed her to use the station phone. Unfortunately, Veronica didn't have much luck with that since she couldn't look up the phone numbers of her credit cards. Veronica instead called her family to let them know what happened to her. Officer Smith had begun working on her case, speaking to the other officers in the department. After given the go to search for the suspect, Officer Smith approached Veronica with the news but paused when she overheard Veronica talking on the phone.

"This was a mistake, I'm just going to come back home. I don't think there's anything the police can do." Veronica said over the phone to her family.

"Excuse me, sorry to interrupt but, I think I might know where to find your purse or at least the person who took it." Veronica immediately hung up the phone without a goodbye, quickly stood up, and shouted,

"Okay, let's go!"

Officer Smith was more excited as she smiled and quickly gathered her things. Officer Smith then walked Veronica out of the office and down the hall. Veronica was thrilled that she had someone so eager to help but she continued to worry and asked,

"Are you new?" Veronica asked with curiosity.

"What do you mean?"

"How long have you been a cop, is what I mean?"

"About three months!" Before Officer Smith and Veronica walked outside, she suggested that Veronica wait in the waiting area. "Listen, my partner and I, we're going to do everything we can to get your purse back. You can wait here, or you can go home, and we will call you if we find anything, but I don't want to get your hopes up."

"No, I'm not going anywhere until I get my purse back."

As the other Officer approached, Veronica felt

more confident when she saw it was a male. She also paid close attention to his nametag, mainly because it also read, Smith. Veronica became even more curious.

"So is everyone here named Officer Smith? Wait, you're the guy in the photo!"

"What photo?" The other Officer asked in confusion.

"I'm sorry, I saw your wedding photo, so you two are married, and you work together? Isn't that against like, the rules or something?"

"Ma'am, do you want to get your purse back or not?" The male Officer asked politely.

Veronica immediately became silent, and the two officers headed out, leaving Veronica inside feeling anxious. While both officers got in the car and started to drive off, the male Officer became curious.

"So Jay, tell me, where are we going?"

"Well do you remember that guy we brought in last week, the one we caught stealing at that convenient store?"

"Yeah what about him?"

"He matched that woman's description, apparently he stole her purse, but this time, we are going to bring him in for good."

It turned out that Officer Smith was right, the same guy they arrested for stealing a week ago, was the same guy who stole Veronica's purse. I guess some people just never learn, but luckily for Veronica, by the time they arrived at what looked like a trap house, the officers were able to catch the man and arrest him. Veronica was relieved when the officers returned to the station with her purse, which still had her house keys, and phone inside. The only thing that was missing was the money, which was a total of 100 dollars, and a few of her credit cards.

While the male Officer was taking the robber into the room for booking, the other Officer was left alone in the waiting area with Veronica. She began to say,

"I hope you learned never to bring your purse to a bus stop in Oakland, you got lucky."

"Yeah I know, I guess I have to start taking an Uber to class."

"You just have to practice using your street smarts, this city is too crazy, and getting crazier."

"Yeah well, I'll never forget about this day, that's

for sure. But thank you. I don't think I've thanked you for your help, and I'm sorry I didn't believe that you could."

"No problem, I like making people think I don't know anything, so when they see me rise to the top, they will be dumbfounded by my success." Both chuckled.

"Well now that I have my purse, I don't have any cash, is it possible for someone to give me a ride home?"

"Of course, I will get one of the officers to give you a ride. Hey, hang in there, it will be okay."

"Thanks, Officer...Smith."

"Call me, Jasmine!" Veronica smiled and began to walk back over to her seat. Jasmine felt sorry for Veronica as she gazed at her stretched out clothing, and pour posture.

"Wait," Jasmine approached and whispered. Listen, I usually don't do this, but I feel bad about what happened to you today. I don't want you to end your night thinking that moving to California was a mistake. My shift ends soon, and I'm going to have dinner with a couple of friends. I can buy you something to eat if you want."

"Why are you so nice?" Veronica questioned.

"I am trying to show you that California isn't all bad and that there's still a few decent human beings left in the world. Plus, you need to make some friends out here." Veronica took a moment to consider Jasmine's offer, and from the growl of her stomach she replied,

"Okay sure, thanks. I am kind of hungry."

Veronica felt relieved that maybe her prayers were being answered. Jasmine wrote down Veronica's address and told her that she would give her a ride to the restaurant in downtown San Francisco. Later that evening, around 8 pm, Jasmine picked Veronica up from her apartment, and she drove them to the restaurant. Veronica enjoyed the views coming into the city from the bridge; how the mountains surrounding the city looked so tall and mysterious.

When they arrived at the restaurant and walked inside, Jasmine's friends, Erika and Nicole, greeted them. Veronica was instantly shocked when she saw Nicole, as she recognized her from earlier in the day. Veronica became speechless and embarrassed.

"What a minute, you're that girl from the bus stop. Oh my God...Oh...my God. Karma is a bitch,"

Nicole said, chuckling aloud while Jasmine and Erika joined in.

"I don't see anything funny," Veronica replied in defense.

"I'm sorry, really. I'm glad you got your purse back," Nicole continued chuckling to herself.

The women then walked over to their table and sat down. As the evening grew into night, the three women had a chance to catch up and also had a chance to get to know Veronica. Nicole being the oldest of the group continually offers her advice to the other women. Though they don't mind, they respect her wisdom, but sometimes it's not always needed. Veronica quickly felt like part of the group and the troubles she faced soon faded away.

One particular relationship in the group began to blossom quickly, and that was the relationship between Veronica and Erika. The two were the youngest and shared similar interests. Veronica was impressed that Erika had a business degree and was part owner of a bar in town. Erika was impressed by Veronica's courage and bluntness. She was also easy on the eyes.

"So, when did you decide that you wanted to study journalism?"

"Well, at first, I was pursuing a career in performing arts. I wanted to be an actress, and I still do, but I found Journalism to be more tangible. Plus, I think being a reporter will be exciting, interviewing people, I don't know, I feel like it's a career that will never get boring. And in a way, I still get to act."

"That's dope. Maybe you can interview me one day."

"Maybe," Veronica smiled.

Erika and Veronica continued their conversation, and her night ended better than it started. Veronica exchanged phone numbers with each of the women, and when she arrived back home, she was all smiles and giggles. Finally feeling accepted was a great feeling. As Veronica got ready for bed, she heard a loud thump coming from the ceiling. At first, she didn't mind it, but the sound continued and grew into an annoyance. Veronica quickly assumed it was her neighbor above, causing the loud ruckus, and she immediately went upstairs to ask them to quiet the noise.

Veronica knocked three times and waited for an answer. The noise stopped for a few seconds and then continued. Veronica became furious and banged on the door until there was an answer. A woman opened the door in shock.

"Excuse me; whatever you're doing in there is extremely loud, and it's keeping me from sleeping." Veronica became nosey as she tried to look into the apartment to see what the commotion was. The woman, standing in front of her, stared in confusion.

"¿Qué?"

"Oh now we're going to play the, I can't speak English card."

The woman spoke in Spanish and pointed to her living room as she tried to explain what she was doing. Veronica looked inside and noticed her artwork. There were beautiful panting's on every wall, and Veronica quickly became amazed.

"Listen, I don't know what you're saying, I don't speak Spanish."

"Come!" The woman motioned for Veronica to come inside so that she could explain what she was doing. Veronica cautiously walked inside, took a look around the living room, and became speechless as she took a closer look at the paintings. They were pastel. One painting, in particular, captivated Veronica. It was of a woman parting the seas and the sky, and through it reveled the galaxies and stars. A woman stood centered with her arms spread out as if she was calling the end of days. Veronica walked closer toward the painting and said,

"Wow, this is beautiful."

"You Like?" The woman approached from behind.

"Yes. Um, me gusta mucho." Veronica pointed and smiled.

"Thank you. Um, no hablo mucho ingles." The woman said to Veronica.

"Well, all though I'm very impressed by your work, is there any way you can work quietly?" The woman didn't understand, and so Veronica reached into her pocket to get her phone.

Veronica translated to the woman that she was being noisy and was keeping her awake. The woman instantly apologized, as she didn't know she was causing a disturbance. The woman offered Veronica water and asked her to have a seat. Veronica was hesitant again because she knew she needed to get up early for class the next day. However, she agreed and sat down. While the woman went to get Veronica a glass of water, she continued to stare at her artwork.

"¿Cual es su nombre?" The woman asked as she handed Veronica a nice ice-cold glass of water.

"I'm sorry?" Veronica was confused and took the glass of water. The woman then sat down next to her.

"Me, Gloria...y tu?" Gloria pointed to herself as she told Veronica her name.

"Ah, okay, sorry, I'm Veronica."

"Veronica, good name." Gloria smiled.

"Thanks." Veronica took a sip of water, and Gloria continued smiling.

Gloria wanted to communicate with Veronica but knew that it would be difficult with their language barrier, so she took out her phone and used her translator. Gloria told Veronica what her painting meant. She explained that her artwork was her theory of a woman being God, and she also believed that God spoke through all of us, revealing the truth about where we came from and where we're going.

Veronica was immediately impressed because not only did Gloria have brains and artistic talents, but she was quite gorgeous. Gloria was androgynous, but yet had her unique style, and she had beautifully high cheekbones to match. Veronica, once again left her worries and frustrations behind as she entertained Gloria in conversation through the night. They both talked about space, time, and their theories of everything. Before Veronica knew it, she was watching the sunrise from the window of Gloria's apartment. Veronica was in complete awe of Gloria, and though she had never been with a woman, she began to entertain the idea of being with Gloria.

Days turned into months, and the months turned into years. During that time, Veronica and Gloria grew closer. Veronica also deepened her friendships with Nicole, Jasmine, and Erika, but Erika most of all. Veronica kept the relationship she was building with Gloria private for a couple of reasons. Veronica wasn't sure if she was ready to explore her sexuality, and the language barrier was a bit of an embarrassment to her. So, Veronica spent most of the time either with Erika or with Gloria. Erika loved the fact that both she and Veronica were single. It made her feel less of a failure for not having a relationship, and less jealous when she was around Jasmine or Nicole. It wasn't until Veronica told Erika about Gloria, that things started to take a different turn in their friendship.

Although Gloria and Veronica hadn't yet made their relationship official, the innuendoes were there, and they both knew that the relationship they were building was more than just a friendship. Veronica began to fall for Gloria, and Gloria the same. At that point, any feelings of embarrassment that Veronica may have had quickly became non-existent. Veronica didn't care what anyone thought of her or her relationship; she just wanted to be happy. Naturally, the first person she told was Erika. Veronica invited Erika to her new apartment in San Francisco. They both sat in the living room and had a glass of wine. Veronica was eager to share the news.

"Alright, what did you need to tell me that couldn't wait until tomorrow?" Erika chucked.

"Do you remember my neighbor, the artist I told you about?"

"Yeah, I think so, the one who doesn't speak English?"

"Yes, but she can speak a little bit of English, anyway, we've sort of been seeing each other for about a year now. We didn't make anything official until the other day. But you were the first person I wanted to tell because I had never been with a woman. I never wanted to be with a woman, but there was something about her, her mind, that captivated me."

Veronica continued to brag about her relationship with Gloria, and how excited she was about it. Though Erika was attentive, all she wanted to do was scream. She knew that she should support her friend and be happy for her, but that wasn't the case. Erika once again felt alone and began to make it about herself. She didn't understand why Veronica didn't mention the relationship sooner, but more importantly, Erika couldn't figure out why it was so hard for her to find love, why Veronica didn't choose her instead. Erika hated how everyone around her seemed to find love so easily.

Later that year, on Christmas Eve, Veronica was invited to Nicole's for Christmas dinner, and naturally, she invited Gloria. Jasmine invited Bobby, and Erika came alone. Everyone shared their successes, personal, work, and relationship. Veronica was a year away from graduating with her Journalism degree, Erika's business was doing well, and Nicole and Jasmine were succeeding in their careers. Everyone seemed to be doing well, but what appeared to be, was not actually what was. Erika played off her jealousy as she tried to get along with Gloria. In the back of Erika's mind, she was brewing up trouble.

Everyone enjoyed a nice dinner, which was prepared by Nicole and Daniel. Halfway through dinner, Erika began translating for Gloria as the group wanted to know details about her and how she and Veronica met. Luckily for Gloria, Erika was fluent in Spanish and able to translate. But also unluckily for her when Erika began to take advantage of her power. Erika would mix up, and confuse the messages between Gloria and Veronica, thus causing an argument to break out.

Erika twisted what compliments Veronica and Gloria had for each other. She got away with it by being the only person in the room who understood what was happening. That was Erika's attempt to break the two of them up. Erika was very smart but also very calculated. Gloria told everyone in her words that she was in love with Veronica, happy to be in her life, and would like to marry her soon. Erika twisted what Gloria said, and told Veronica and everyone else in the room that Gloria loved

Veronica, but didn't see herself in a monogamous relationship. Erika went on to further lie, and say that Gloria was living a polygamous lifestyle. Veronica immediately became upset and questioned Gloria, but Gloria didn't understand why Veronica was upset by her comment.

Everyone in the room looked confused, and Gloria asked Erika what the problem was. Erika then came up with another lie and told Gloria that Veronica wasn't ready to live a monogamous lifestyle, and felt pressured by her. The back and forth between Gloria and Veronica confused everyone, except Erika. Eventually, Veronica stormed off and left Gloria sitting alone with the rest of the group. Erika knew just what she needed to do next.

As the evening ended, and everyone started to go home, Erika offered Gloria a ride. Gloria accepted and often tried to call Veronica, but there wasn't an answer. Gloria was devastated the rest of the night, and when Erika dropped her off, she asked if she could come inside. Gloria didn't think anything of it, and she agreed. While inside, Gloria offered Erika a glass of water. Erika accepted and took a look around her living room. She was also amazed by the artwork on Gloria's wall and began to speak to Gloria in her native tongue.

"You did all this by yourself?"

"Yeah, it's nothing," Gloria said and flopped down on the sofa.

"Why are you so bummed out? You don't need Veronica. I bet you and I could get along much better. I want the same things as you." Erika said as she sat close to Gloria.

"I'm not interested. I love Veronica."

"Fuck, Veronica, okay. What does she have that I don't?"

"My heart! I think you should leave." Gloria stood up, and walked over towards the door, motioning for Erika to leave, but she just continued to stay seated on the sofa and said,

"I'm not going anywhere; I haven't been here long enough. Besides, you might change your mind."

Erika knew that by morning, Veronica would contact Gloria wanting to talk. Erika wanted Veronica to catch her inside Gloria's apartment, hoping that she could convince Veronica that she and Gloria had sex, and in her mind, it would be the icing on the cake to break them up for good. Erika never had any intentions of sleeping with Gloria; Erika wasn't even attracted to Gloria. Her mind was so twisted, and she was so focused on breaking the two of them up, that she hadn't considered the consequences, the pain that it would cause for Veronica.

Erika never left that night and convinced Gloria to let her crash on the couch. Sure enough, as planned, Veronica came banging on the door the next morning. When Erika opened the door, looking a mess, and topless, acting as if she was drunk, Veronica barged her way inside and shouted,

"Gloria!" Gloria heard Veronica's cry, came rushing out of her room and approached.

"¿Qué? Mi amor..."

"Don't mi amor me. Did you two have sex last night?" Veronica asked, and Erika quickly interrupted.

"We did! You left, what was she supposed to do, you broke her heart."

"I'm not talking to you, fuck you. Gloria, did you fuck her?" Veronica motioned with her hands. Gloria quickly shook her head and swore that they didn't have sex, however,

Veronica couldn't believe the truth, and instead stormed away back to her apartment.

Gloria chased after her trying to explain everything that happened. Veronica just wasn't convinced that they didn't have sex. But even so, Veronica would rather be with Gloria than not, and her heart hurt too much to be apart another day. As she and Gloria stood at the front of Veronica's door, Gloria got down on one knee. She pleaded for her forgiveness and proposed. Erika watched from the top of the staircase in fury as Veronica accepted her proposal.

That was it; Erika's plan was ruined. She not only lost the game, but she lost a friend that day as well. That day stayed in Veronica's mind like growing cancer, just eating away at her. Every time Veronica would take a deep long look at Gloria, she'd wonder if her and Erika ever crossed that line.

Back to the present day, as Veronica reminisced on her past ten years ago, she smiled and kissed Gloria on the cheek. Of course, Gloria woke from feeling Veronica's soft lips against her cheek and smiled while her eyes were barely cracked open. It was 3:45 in the morning, after all.

"¿Qué?" Gloria said softly.

"Nothing, I was just thinking. Go back to sleep." Veronica stood up and got ready to leave. But before she made her way out of the room, Gloria stopped her by saying,

"I love you!" Veronica turned around, smiled, and replied,

"Yo También te quiero."

5

Erika

It's been almost a week since Erika was arrested and awaiting her trial. She struggled to accept the actions that brought her into this place of darkness and disgust. Erika would lay in her cell on a cot in a room with three other women. Embarrassed to get up to use the restroom, she'd lay there with a bladder on the verge of eruption. The room was cold, which did not make it any better. It was just moments before a prison guard entered the room and called her name,

"Erika, you have a visitor."

Erika quickly hopped out of bed, and ran to the guard,

"I've been holding it since last night, please, can I use a private restroom?"

"Unfortunately, this is not a hotel. If you need to use the restroom, I suggest that you do it here." The guard stood still, emotionless, while Erika turned around to quickly release her bladder. A minute later, after relieving herself, Erika stood up in slight pain to follow the guard. Erika then walked into a room where she saw a familiar face, one she hadn't seen in a couple of days. Erika was thrilled but also troubled at the same time. She flopped down in the chair in front of her,

"Nicole, what's going on, I haven't seen you in like three or four days."

"I know, I'm sorry, I was trying to sort through everything. This case, it's not looking too good," Nicole sighed in sadness.

"What do you mean it's not looking too good? You're a damn lawyer, you don't lose cases, and now you want to give up on me because I'm what, disposable because you're not getting paid?" Erika said in frustration as she folded her arms.

"What! How dare you say that to me? I've been working my ass off day and night."

"You've been working your ass off but not on my damn case. What woman is it this week?"

"And that right there, that's part of the reason why I haven't been by." The room quickly heated up between the two of them. Nicole didn't understand why Erika spoke to her with such disrespect, and Erika didn't understand why Nicole wasn't trying hard enough to get her out of jail.

"Don't push the one person away who still has your back. I'm not the one who strangled my girlfriend to death! You need to take responsibility for your actions and stop acting like you can go around doing whatever the hell you want as if you'll never have to suffer any kind of consequence. Jasmine and Veronica don't know what's in your files, but I do, and that's what's hurting you, not me!"

"What did you find in my files, Nicole?" Nicole paused before she continued to speak, afraid of what the truth would reveal.

"Why don't you tell me everything I need to know this time, and maybe I can help you."

Erika stared back at Nicole; afraid to share the truth about her life, fearful of what Nicole would think of her if she confirmed what was in those files. Erika began to take a look into herself, into her past. Her earliest memories were the best, and those memories were what she held closest to her heart. Without those first childhood memories, Erika believed she would be borderline psychopathic if she wasn't already.

Erika began to remember her childhood and how things were before she became the person she is today, broken, lost, and empty. In school, Erika was a sweetheart. Do you remember those students who were called Teacher's Pet? Well, that was Erika. She always had a smile on her face, and she enjoyed making other people smile. It lit something bright inside her soul, something that couldn't be explained. If there was one thing her soul clung to the most, it was the idea of being loved. Since Erika was a child, that's all she ever wanted. Although she had lots of love to give to others, and her soul shined bright, it seemed darkness always found a way of attaching itself and dimming her light.

When in middle school, and even in high school, Erika would surround herself with people she thought would be her friends. However, Erika learned that they only took from her, dimming her light even more. Erika was 15 when she came out of the closet as gay. Erika never understood why she had feelings toward the same sex. Erika believed and was taught that homosexuality was a sin. Though she feared sin, she couldn't fight her true feelings. The tingling sensations she would get just from setting close to a girl that she fancied, or how her stomach filled with butterflies. Those were feelings she'd always felt toward the same sex. When Erika had her first kiss at 16, it was as if her whole body from head to toe got sent an electrical charge. Erika never needed to question her sexuality; she knew exactly who she was.

When Erika turned 18, her mother was diagnosed with schizophrenia. Erika never understood why sometimes her mother would have conversations with herself or loud outbursts from anger. It wasn't until Erika secretly spoke to a doctor about her mother's condition, and convinced her mother to see a professional, that they could get her treated for the disease. Erika's father left when she was just 12 years old, and she never heard from or saw him again. Erika came from a big family and had lots of aunts and uncles. However, they didn't have much of a relationship with her or her mother. So, Erika considered her mother as her only family. Things were going great after her mother got treated. The only downside was making sure that her mother could continue taking her medications. Erika's mother had a couple of instances where she'd stop taking her medications for some time, and her symptoms would creep right back to the surface.

When Erika was 19, her mother committed suicide. Erika believed it was due to her forgetting to take her medication or the voices that carried her away to a night of permanent sleep. Erika's pride and anger wouldn't allow her to contact her family, as she partly blamed them for her mother's death. Erika was already enrolled in college and was on the verge of dropping out after coming back from bereavement leave. But then she met Jasmine. Erika was going to school to study business, and she and Jasmine shared the same law class.

Erika had a way of blocking out her pain and focusing it on other people. Erika knew that she didn't want to drop out of college, so she tried to push through the pain. Erika got used to being hurt in life, and having things taken away from her; she learned to bury her pain, but never to heal from it. Erika was a complete mess her first day back since her mother's funeral. She was in a rush to get to class as she was running late. Erika stormed down the halls, out of breath, and suddenly fell to the ground. Thinking she could return to class as if everything was fine, she couldn't. So, Erika ran into the restroom, into a stall, and began to weep. Erika prayed and asked, "Why me, why does my life have to be filled with pain and sorrow, when will it end?"

Erika didn't understand why she was dealt a horrible hand in life, what was the meaning, the purpose. Was she meant to be the Universe's joke? Erika thought of ending her life that day, she'd come up with a plan to reunite with her mother, but as quickly as the thought came to be, she heard someone enter the restroom. And that's of course, when she met Jasmine. Erika was shocked by how kind and caring she was. Erika was used to being treated rudely, inhumane, so it surprised her when someone shed a bit of light back towards her.

Erika naturally became attached to Jasmine; she was the only friend, the only person that she had. Over time, Erika wanted to put a Band-Aid over her pain by meeting someone new, someone special. Only to Erika's disappointment, Jasmine was not only straight, but she was in a relationship with Bobby. Though Erika was disappointed that Jasmine could not romantically mend her pain, she was still glad to have her as a friend.

When Erika finished school and got her business degree, she later sought advice from a lawyer. That's when she met Nicole, and Erika's friendship circle quickly widened. Jasmine, Erika, and Nicole became like the three musketeers. As the years passed, Erika slowly covered up the pain that she'd endured in life. Erika band-aided the loss of her mother, the heartbreaks, and how her bright light became a dim shadow in her mind. Erika never sought help from a therapist until she had a conversation with Nicole.

Erika had gotten into yet another draining relationship, which would soon burn out the rest of her light. The interesting thing about Erika was, although she was used to being betrayed by other people, she still had a slither of hope that maybe the next person would treat her right. When Erika was around 23 years of age, she met a beautiful young woman by the name of Tessa. Tessa had long straight brunette hair, dimples that went deep for miles, and bright green eyes. Tessa was a beauty, and often Erika felt that she wasn't good enough to be with a girl like her. She often questioned, "Why is she with me?" Erika didn't realize just how much of herself she was giving, only to be with Tessa.

Erika would go out of her way, buying Tessa lunches and dinners, as she'd often show up to Tessa's job to surprise her. Tessa never did the same in return, but Erika didn't care; she was just happy as she thought she was loved in return. Tessa worked at a supermarket and was going to school full time to be an engineer. Tessa had looks, but she was also brilliant. There were times when Erika couldn't afford to pay for both herself and Tessa to eat, so she'd choose to feed Tessa over herself. Erika would, of course, eat a bowl of noodles, or a sandwich when she got home. Erika wanted and needed Tessa's approval. Although Erika did these things, it still wasn't enough.

It wasn't until one day when Tessa invited Erika to go to a bonfire gathering in the woods, that Erika had a change of heart. Erika had never been to the woods or camping for that matter, but she was excited to go. Erika was invited to Muir

Woods, just north of San Francisco. The nice part about these woods, they were only an hour and a half hike to the beach. The plan was that they'd all start in a hike, and end at the beach for the bonfire. Oddly enough, although Erika lived in San Francisco/Oakland all of her life, she'd only been to the beach a total of 10 times. It wasn't that she didn't enjoy the water, but she had so much going on in life that she barely had time to catch the ocean breeze.

Erika soon found out that she wasn't enjoying her life at all, but she was slowly giving it away. Earlier that day, Erika and Tessa were getting ready for their camping trip. Erika often had Tessa over, and this was one of those mornings. Erika informed her friends, Nicole and Jasmine, letting them know where she'd be going just in case she got stranded out in the woods. Erika was excited as she got ready and brushed her teeth, Tessa joined,

"Hey babe, how did you sleep?"

"I always sleep nicely with you in my arms," Erika smiled.

"That's what I like to hear!" Tessa kissed Erika on the cheek, and she invited herself to share the sink.

"I can't wait for you to meet my friends," Tessa said with a mouth full of toothpaste."

"I hope they like me, I'm nervous."

"Don't be; they will love you."

Later that day, Erika and Tessa got on the road to meet Tessa's friends at Muir Woods. Luckily for them, it wasn't a far drive coming from South San Francisco. Erika drove in her white 1997 Toyota corolla, and Tessa relaxed with her sunglasses on her face, taking in the breeze from the ocean as they crossed the Golden Gate Bridge. It would be another 20 minutes before they'd reach the woods.

When they finally arrived, Tessa hopped out of the car in excitement and greeted her three friends. Jerry was the tallest of the bunch and wore a mid-length scruffy beard with hair gold like honey. Adam was tall and slim and wore a closely shaven goatee and mustache with dark brown hair. Then there was Bryan. Bryan was short, quiet, had a buzz cut, and bad acne. All three guys wore similar workout clothing, and they immediately greeted Erika when she stepped out of the car.

"Hey, I'm Adam!" Adam reached out his hand to shake Erika's.

"Hi, I'm Erika, nice to meet you," Erika smiled and greeted the other two gentlemen.

They were each very welcoming and relaxed; you could tell that they smoked a little beforehand. Erika didn't mind; she was happy to be apart of something, making new friends, so she thought. The five of them headed off for their hike down to the beach. It was around 3 pm when everyone started hiking. With this being the fall time of year, they knew they would be losing the sunlight in a couple of hours.

"So, how long have you guys known each other?" Jerry asked.

"I'd say about three months, not that long," Erika replied and smiled at Tessa.

"And you guys just hit it off, how did you two meet?" Adam asked with curiosity.

"She didn't tell you?" Erika replied in confusion.

"There's a lot that Tessa doesn't tell us. We only found out about you a week ago," Bryan replied.

"Whoa, you guys know I'm private, and I wanted to make sure she would stick around before I went telling everyone," Tessa said in defense.

"Sure, say what you want, dude. If I had a woman

as hot as her, I would have been texting like dude, check her out, she's hot and black, Cha-Ching."

Erika became uncomfortable by Bryan's comment, and they each stopped and stared.

"What the fuck is wrong with you, Bryan?" Adam replied.

"I'm just messing around."

The group continued walking down the path, and Tessa apologized to Erika for Bryan's comment. As they continued hiking through the woods, Erika became curious about Tessa's relationship with the guys.

"So, how did you guys meet Tessa? I thought when she said I'd be meeting her friends that they'd be..."

"Girls?" Adam said while chuckling to himself.

"Well yeah."

"Okay, Well, Jerry and Tessa were once an item, if you didn't already know..."

"Wait, you didn't tell me that one of your friends was your ex." Erika quickly became upset and embarrassed.

"Babe, it's not a big deal, we took a break last year, I told Jerry that I was interested in woman, and he gave me the space I needed. You don't need to be jealous."

"It's not about being jealous, but I feel stupid. Wait, you said taking a break, so are you guys still together?" Erika stared back and forth between Jerry and Tessa while Adam and Bryan watched.

"We're not together, there's no need to worry," Jerry said plainly and headed off down the trail.

"I promise, there's nothing to worry about." Tessa said as she tried to reassure Erika.

Tessa grabbed Erika by the hand, and they followed behind Jerry, Adam, and Bryan. The hike was quiet the rest of the way until the group reached the beach. Adam and Bryan got started on the bonfire while Erika, Tessa, and Jerry conversed.

"Listen, I don't want this to be awkward for you, and I honestly thought Tessa would have told you before bringing you out here. Maybe she was afraid that if she told you, you wouldn't come." Jerry said in Tessa's defense.

"No, don't worry about it. I came to have a good time so, let's have a good time!" Erika smiled and walked closer towards the beach. Erika tried to hide her true feelings because she knew that she was already there and didn't want to cause a scene by leaving. Jerry went to help Adam and Bryan, while Tessa followed Erika.

"I'm sorry I didn't tell you before, it's just, Jerry and I were friends before we got in a relationship. But I am here with you."

"Do you still have feelings for him?"

"What?" Tessa asked in confusion.

"Do you have feelings, romantic feelings for Jerry?"

"N-No, not anymore. Can we please just enjoy all of this, the waves, and the view?"

Erika nodded yes, although she still didn't believe what Tessa was telling her. Erika put on a brave face and tried her best to enjoy herself. It wasn't until later that evening when darkness fell that the night took an ugly turn.

Erika often caught Bryan gazing in her direction, which made her feel uncomfortable, but mostly because she didn't know how to take it. Erika didn't know if he was just curious about her, maybe he'd never been around a person of color before, or perhaps he did have a crush. Either way, Erika kept her focus on Tessa and her eyes on Jerry. Erika watched to see if she could catch him in a gaze staring at Tessa, or if his body language suggested more than a friendship. Erika worried herself as she tried to catch Tessa and Jerry in a lie, which turned her night into a nightmare. They each then sat around the campfire and decided to play a game to break the ice.

"Let's play, Two Truths and a Lie." Adam suggested as the group gawked in confusion.

"What's that?" Tessa asked.

"So the way this works, we each tell two truths about ourselves, and one lie. The objective is to guess which is the lie, and if we guess correctly, you gotta take a sip." Adam said as they each sat with a beer in their hands.

"Alright, let's do it," Tessa eagerly said.

"I'll go first," Bryan shouted impatiently. "I love my mom. I got drunk last night, and...I- slept with my best friend." Everyone became quiet as they tried to guess.

"Well I'm your best friend, and I know for damn sure that we didn't have sex, and you're pretty much drunk every night, so I'm going to guess you hate your fucking mom."

"Cha Ching! I hate that bitch!" Bryan laughed to himself and took a sip of his beer.

"Why do you hate your mom?" Erika asked in confusion.

"Because she abandoned me when I was five and ran off with some creep."

"Okay, my turn! Tessa awkwardly interrupted. "I was born with eleven toes, I kissed my cousin with tongue when I was a kid, and I' m... I'm in love with my girlfriend." Tessa smiled at Erika as she tried to cheer her up. Erika smiled back, and the guys in the group stared in confusion.

"So, was this a girl cousin or a guy cousin?" Jerry asked.

"Dude does it matter? She French kissed her cousin!" Adam said in disgust.

"Okay! Don't act like you guys are so innocent, I'm sure there's worse things you have done."

"I don't know incest is taking it far," Bryan said as he chuckled."

"Whatever, are we playing the game or not," asked Tessa.

"Yeah... I'm going to guess that since you just admitted kissing your cousin was true, and the way you smiled when you said you were in love with Erika, must be true, I'm going to guess that you don't have 11 toes." Jerry smiled.

"You got me! Okay, you're turn." Tessa said as she took a sip of her beer.

"Alright, uh, my favorite singer of all time is Davy Jones, I had sex with the lead singer of a band last week, and I'm still in love with my ex.

Everyone became quiet and immediately turned to Tessa and then stared at Erika.

"I'm going to guess that you wouldn't be an idiot and admit that you love your ex while she's here with her new girlfriend, I'm going to say that was the lie." Tessa said in frustration as she stared at Jerry, who became slightly offended.

"Yeah, obviously, that was the lie."

Later on, as the night grew darker, and the fire burned brighter, they each decided to settle into their tents. Erika had a weak bladder and needed to relieve herself. Jerry suggested a good spot for her to do so. It was about half a mile away from camp, which took Erika about ten minutes to walk. Of course, she wasn't concerned about bears or anything else; she immediately headed deeper into the woods. Once Erika found a spot, she pulled down her pants and relieved herself. Only she did not know that Bryan had followed behind.

"Hey!" Bryan smiled.

"Jesus! What are you doing? You scared me."

"I'm sorry, I was just making sure that you were okay. These woods can be pretty dangerous when you're out here alone."

"Thanks, but I can take care of myself." Erika quickly pulled up her pants and tried to hurry off, but Bryan grabbed her by the arm and stopped her.

"Wait a minute, why don't we have a chat, get to know each other better. Your ass is looking very sexy in those yoga pants."

"They are joggers first off all, and second, let go of my arm. I don't know what your problem is, but I'm very much gay and uninterested."

"What you want doesn't matter, not here, not in these woods. Only predators survive out here."

Erika quickly became threatened by Bryan's remark and tried to run; however, Bryan was too quick to let her go. Although Bryan was the shortest of the guys in the group, he was the most athletic. Bryan grabbed Erika by the ponytail and slammed her to the ground face down. He quickly got on top of her as he ripped her clothes and unfastened his pants. Bryan then forced himself inside Erika while she cried out, "Stop! Please!"

Erika tried to fight him off, but as he straddled behind, pressing her head into the dirt, Erika was powerless.

Erika was a sweet child who only wanted to be loved. She lost her mother and didn't have a family, not any family who cared enough to look for her anyway. While Erika was being raped in the middle of the woods without a soul to help, she was sure she would die. At one point, Erika hoped that she would die so that her misery on Earth would finally come to an end. Bryan soon finished, and slowly got up.

What a high he felt, while he slowly zipped up his pants. Erika would lay there in tears, afraid to move, afraid to speak as she inhaled the dirt from the ground. Bryan then kneeled, looked Erika in the eye and said,

"I'm going to tell Tessa and the others that you got upset and left. What you're going to do is get in your car, drive back home, and never return here again. You won't even call Tessa again, she doesn't love you, and she's probably fucking Jerry in the tent right now. If you do come back, I will kill you! I will spot you coming back to camp before anyone else. You got me? Do not come back here."

Bryan got up and then spit on Erika's face. He walked away, leaving her there alone in the woods. It wasn't until morning that Erika had the mental strength to get up. Erika's face was covered in dirt, and tiny bugs had crawled all over her legs. She then wiped away the dirt and dusted off the bugs as she stood up and pulled up her pants. But instead of heeding to Bryan's threat, she went back to camp. Erika waited until she saw Bryan go out alone into the woods, and she quietly followed.

Bryan walked over by a tree and relieved himself of his bladder. It was still pretty early in the morning, so Bryan was still half asleep, which gave Erika the advantage. Erika quietly searched for something that she could use to strike him in the skull. To her surprise, she found a mid-sized rock that rested perfectly in her hand. Erika crept up behind Bryan, and before he could zip up his pants, Erika struck him in the head with the rock. Bryan quickly turned around in confusion and laid his eyes on Erika. He tried to grab her, but she quickly knocked him to the ground with another blow the head.

This time, Erika straddled Bryan and struck him repeatedly until he was no longer conscious.

Bryan's face was completely disfigured, and blood poured out from his temple like a stream of water. Erika quickly got up and ran. She ran as far and as fast as she could with the rock in her hand. Erika then noticed a river, and tossed the rock into the water, staying just long enough to hear it splash. Erika continued running until she reached her car, which was parked in a parking lot near the woods. Erika cried a river of tears as she rushed into her car and shouted from the pain that she endured.

Erika wondered to herself, *Why is it okay for people to treat me like this, why was I put on this planet to be a punching bag, to be unlovable?* Erika didn't understand what it was that she did to deserve the torture. Erika immediately thought to call her mother to tell her what happened. As quickly as Erika picked up her phone to dial her mother's number, she remembered her mother wouldn't be there on the other end to answer. Erika once again felt alone in the world and continued to weep. The one person she needed, who she wished she could cry to, was no longer alive. Erika said to herself,

I wish I could tell you all the pain I've been through, all the abuse, how my life is completely miserable. I

wish that I could cry to you and tell you that I was raped last night, but I can't. Erika sat in her car a few more moments until she heard shouting from a distance and realized she needed to get as far away from there as possible. Erika drove away in tears and swore to never get into another relationship again. Her heart, however, would soon break that promise, as she later met Evangeline.

Fast forward to the present day, Erika sat across from Nicole who was in tears from hearing her story. Erika never told a soul about what happened to her in those woods until now, not even her therapist knew. The only details she gave to her therapist was that she remembered beating Bryan with a rock, but wasn't sure of what happened to him. Nicole stared at Erika feeling her pain.

"Erika, why didn't you tell me any of this before?"

"I don't know. It doesn't matter. You want me to say that I feel bad for the things that I've done, but I don't feel a damn thing. After all the hell I've been through? It's not okay to kill, but why is it okay to have your spirit beaten up little by little until there's nothing left? To be raped, bullied, objectified, a victim of racism, why are those things okay?"

"I'm sorry that I wasn't there for you, the way that you needed me to be. And I know that it's hard, not having your mother in your life, but I don't want you to give up on yourself."

"I haven't given up, it's everyone else who has given up on me," Erika said.

"If they can tie you to that murder, I'm not sure that I'll be able to prove insanity. The judge will see it as first-degree murder, and you will go to prison. But I'm going to fight as hard as I can for you, I promise!" Erika stared at Nicole, almost daydreaming like, on the verge of crying and asked,

"Do you think my mom still loves me?"

"Oh honey...of course she does, a love like that is unconditional!"

6

Freedom

Months have passed, and Nicole has been studying Erika's case day and night. It was midnight, and Nicole was still trying to figure out how she could convince the judge to go lightly on Erika, to convince the judge that Erika had some sort of mental illness. Nicole worried herself to death, wondering how she would defend Erika's actions. To distract herself from the stress of the case, Nicole would chat with Robyn. They spoke every night since Nicole worked up the nerve to call that one early morning. Robyn has been busy herself, working as a family law attorney. The two of them weren't able to catch up in person until this particular night when Nicole invited Robyn over.

Daniel was away for the weekend at a school event, and the kids were asleep. Nicole paced her living room floor until Robyn arrived. Suddenly, there was a knock at the door, and Nicole rushed to answer but took a moment to get herself together before answering.

"Hi, thanks for coming by," Nicole smiled.

"No, I'm glad you called." Robyn walked inside, and Nicole offered her something to drink.

"Thanks, I'm fine for now. What's all this?" Robyn took a look at Nicole's paperwork, spread out all over the coffee table in the living room.

"I'm working on a case for my friend Erika."

"Oh right, is she the friend who got arrested for killing her girlfriend?"

"Yes, unfortunately. But here, have a seat!" Nicole rushed to clean up the papers that she had spread out on the table, and she neatly put them away. Robyn glared at Nicole with a smile.

"I'm just amazed. You're still just as beautiful as you were the last time I saw you, if not more."

Nicole awkwardly sat down next to Robyn and crossed her legs.

"Thank you! I like the new look." Nicole admired Robyn's new hair cut, which she wore short and curly, just barely touching her neck. Both Nicole and Robyn didn't know where to begin, what to say. They both smiled, admiring one another. Robyn took a glance around the living room. She quickly noticed Nicole's wedding and family photos that rested on top of the fireplace.

"You have a beautiful family. That's Daniel, I'm guessing?" Robyn asked.

"Thank you, and yes, that would be Daniel."

Robyn became saddened, though she tried not to show it, Nicole was able to read her body language well.

"Listen, I want to apologize for letting you walk away and not fighting to keep you in my life. There hasn't been a day where I don't regret the choices I've made. I miss you all the time," Nicole softly said.

"It's okay, we were both young, and now you have this amazing life, career, and family. There's nothing to be sorry for." Robyn tried to play it cool;

she tried to be supportive of Nicole's decisions. But Nicole knew her better than she realized.

"You said that whenever I'm ready to be myself..." Nicole became emotional as she tried to fight back her tears. "You said, whenever I'm ready to love myself for who I am, to give you a call. Robyn, I know I might be a decade or more too late, but I'm ready. I want to be free."

Nicole and Robyn had an emotional exchange as they continued their conversation.

The next morning, Jasmine and Bobby were at home having yet another one of their fights. Bobby's tactic was to make Jasmine jealous because he could sense a sort of distance coming from her. Jasmine has had enough at this point and was trying to separate from the marriage of which she trapped herself. While the two were getting ready in their bedroom, Bobby pretended to text another woman on his phone. Bobby would smile and make annoying little chuckles. Jasmine tried to converse with him about her feelings, but he ignored her as he continued to look down at his phone.

Jasmine became furious, and she snatched the

phone right out of his hands and threw it on the bed beside them. Bobby then SMACKED Jasmine, leaving her surprised, almost losing her balance. She then punched Bobby in the throat, causing him to lose his balance and fall. Jasmine stormed out of the room, and Bobby got himself together to chase after her. As Jasmine headed down the stairs, Bobby followed and offered an apology, but his apology wasn't good enough. Jasmine continued with her morning routine as she packed her lunch, but also made it clear that she wouldn't continue to put up with his behavior.

"Bobby, I'm tired of fighting you, literally. I can't do it anymore, and you refuse to get professional help."

"What are you talking about? You started it by snatching my phone out of my hand."

"So that makes slapping me, okay?"

"You hit me back, you punched me in my damn throat," Bobby shouted.

"Because you...you know what, you can continue living in this false world all by yourself, I'm done."

Jasmine went to finish packing her lunch and walked out of the kitchen. Bobby was left with his thoughts, feeling as though he was losing his power and control over her. Bobby didn't know what to do without Jasmine in his life; he depended on her so much over the years, caused him to lose his sense of self. That fueled Bobby's anger, and he went after Jasmine, catching her before she walked out of the front door.

"You can't just give up on me, on us. Look I'm sorry okay, is that what you want to hear, will that make you stay?"

"At this point, Bobby, nothing you say will make me stay. I should have left your ass years ago." Jasmine went to grab her keys, which were hanging up by the door. Before Jasmine could take a step outside, Bobby grabbed her by the hair, pulling her back inside, shoving her to the ground. Jasmine quickly got up, took her keys, and scratched Bobby along the side of his face causing the skin to rip open. Jasmine attempted to leave again, but Bobby went after her, pushing her back against the door as he grabbed her neck and began choking her.

"Should I do you like your friend did her dead girlfriend? Will that make you stay?"

Jasmine tried to break free from Bobby's hold, but the more she fought, the tighter he squeezed.

It wasn't until Jasmine was red in the face that he finally released his grip, causing her to fall to the ground in tears. Gasping for breath, Jasmine looked up at Bobby, who was in full rage. Jasmine couldn't understand why she allowed herself to stay in such an abusive relationship for so long.

Jasmine worried if he would kill her; instead, he slowly walked out of the front door. Jasmine cried alone on the ground, wondering what she should do. Jasmine knew she didn't have many options; at least that's what she thought. She built her home there with Bobby; whether it was an abusive home or not, Jasmine was terrified over the idea of starting over, though, at the same time, she knew she couldn't continue down this road.

Later on that morning, Nicole was preparing for Erika's trial. Robyn stayed the night to offer her support, and to help calm Nicole's worries; however, Nicole just worried even more. She had already dropped Jeremiah and Ruth off at school, and Robyn took it upon herself to cook the two of them breakfast. Nicole walked into the kitchen to the smell of scrambled eggs and bacon.

"Hey, I hope you don't mind. I figured you would need something to eat."

"No, I don't mind at all, it smells delicious in here." Nicole walked over to Robyn and kissed her on her cheek. Robyn fixed them both a plate, and poured two glasses of orange juice, and even had a pot of coffee ready to go. The two sat down at the table and indulged themselves.

"So, are you ready for today?" Robyn asked after taking a small bite of egg.

"No, but I have no choice but to be."

"I'm sure everything will work out, Nicki."

"Yeah, it just may not work out the way we want it to."

While Nicole and Robyn were enjoying their breakfast, they heard banging on the door that startled them. Nicole got up, reassured Robyn that everything was okay, and went to answer the door. When Nicole saw Jasmine standing on the other side with bruises all over her face and neck, she became flabbergasted.

"Oh my God, did he do this to you?" Jasmine walked inside with her left eye swollen and a busted lip. "Jesus Christ, come sit down, what the hell happened?" Nicole continued talking, and Jasmine sat down in the living room on the sofa. Then Nicole rushed to get her an iced towel. Robyn noticed, got up from the kitchen table, and walked into the living room.

Robyn was shocked and saddened when she saw Jasmine's bruises, and instantly went to tell Nicole that she would leave to give the two of them privacy.

"No, you don't have to leave," Nicole said.

"It's okay. I will call you later." Robyn approached Jasmine on her way out, and said,

"I know that we don't know each other, but whoever did this to you does not deserve to be in your life." Robyn then walked towards the door, and Nicole stopped her.

"You didn't even finish your breakfast."

"Finish the rest for me."

Robyn left, giving the two of them privacy so that Jasmine could feel more comfortable to tell Nicole what happened to her. Nicole sat next to Jasmine, and she applied the ice towel to her face.

"Jasmine, when are you going to leave him?"

"I don't know." Jasmine cried out. "I know I need to leave him, but where am I going to go?"

"You can stay here with me until you can get your place."

"Girl, I don't even know how much longer you

will be staying here, with the number of women you have coming in and out of here. Eventually, Daniel will find out. That's just drama I'm not trying to be apart of, no offense."

"No, none taken. But, you can't keep putting yourself through *this*, drama."

"Why not, I've been putting up with it for all these years, what could a couple more hurt?"

"I don't care what you say, you're not going back to that house, you're going to stay here and your neck, my God, there's only a matter of time before he kills you or vise versa."

"And when Daniel finds out about these women, we will both be on the streets." Jasmine took the ice towel from Nicole and applied it to her lips.

"That's not going to happen. Daniel won't find out because I'm going to end it. My friends need me right now, and it's selfish of me to think about my love life or the lack of one."

"You're just using us as an excuse so you don't have to deal with your feelings. You cannot do that. You are a lesbian; you need to be honest with Daniel and tell him the truth."

"Don't worry about me, if either one of us needs

to take any action right now, a blind person could clearly see that it's you."

"Shut up," Jasmine painfully laughed.

Later that day, it was almost time for Erika's trial. Veronica was getting ready, although she initially didn't want to go, Nicole convinced her to show up for support. Veronica was still holding on to the grudge she built against Erika years ago. One thing about Veronica, she can hold a grudge to the death, but she doesn't realize that by punishing others, she's also punishing herself. Holding herself hostage from moving on.

While Veronica got dressed in the mirror, she heard the phone ring, and quickly went over to answer.

"You are receiving a collect call from an inmate at the San Francisco county jail; please press one to accept."

Veronica's heart dropped as she knew who would be on the other end. Veronica almost hung up the call until the machine repeated the message, and she then accepted the call. For a moment there was silence on the phone. Neither one of them knew exactly where to start or what to say. Erika began talking,

"Thank you for taking my call."

"What do you want, Erika?"

"I just wanted to say...I just wanted to say that I'm sorry for everything." Erika's voice cracked as she tried to offer Veronica an apology. Veronica, however, wasn't in the mood to hear it. Or at least, her pride wasn't ready to allow her to.

"It's hard for me to believe that you would be sorry for anything. Shouldn't you be getting ready for your trial?"

"There's not much for me to get ready for. I eat, shit, and sleep all in the same room."

"Listen, I don't know what you want me to say. What you did was fucked up, I don't see how you can sleep at night knowing you took another life."

"I don't sleep at night, actually, and I didn't call to argue. I'm trying to make peace with the decisions that I've made, but before I do, I need to know that you can forgive me. You're holding on to anger that doesn't hurt me. What hurts me is knowing that you can't move on; you're not free."

"This is coming from the woman who is about to spend her life in prison."

"Are you mad at me for what I did to you years ago, or are you mad at me for leaving you again. What I've done doesn't have anything to do with you, and it doesn't mean that I never really cared for you or loved you because I did, and I still do. We were once best friends." Veronica began to tear up; she didn't want Erika to know, so she sobbed in silence. Erika went on to say,

"I think that's it. Veronica, I have to go, but I want you to know I love you." There was a short pause and Veronica then quickly said,

"Well, I don't love you."

Veronica hung up the phone as she let her emotions get the best of her. Veronica didn't realize until Erika said it, that she felt betrayed and felt that Erika was never truly genuine with her, that she never really was her friend. Later, Nicole, Jasmine, and Veronica arrived at the courthouse. Nicole wanted to meet with her friends to prepare them both for what they might hear in court. Nicole knew things about Erika that the other two women didn't know. They each met upstairs in the hallway; the courtroom was just a couple feet away. Jasmine was dressed in all black. She wore sunglasses to cover her bruised eye, and a scarf over her head and neck to cover the rest of her bruises.

"Hey, did you guys ride together, why didn't I

get invited to the Uber pool?" Veronica said as she stared at Nicole and then Jasmine.

"And why the hell are you in here dressed like Mother Teresa? Are you hiding from someone?"

"No, I'm not, I just thought I'd try a new look. Plus, I got my eyes dilated this morning."

"When at 6 o'clock?" Veronica was skeptical and continued to ask, "Did you and Bobby get into another fight?"

Veronica knew that there wasn't any chance that Jasmine could have had an eye appointment, mainly because it was 10 am when they arrived.

"We're not here for my marriage problems; we are here for Erika." Jasmine said and then proceeded to walk inside the courtroom. Before Jasmine made it inside, Nicole stopped her, and Veronica.

"Listen, I don't think you two are ready for what's about to go down in there."

"Oh come on, I already know she's going to try and get off with some sad story," Veronica said as she rolled her eyes.

"I'm serious. There are things about Erika that you both don't know, things that will be brought up, and discussed in that courtroom. I just want you to be ready."

Veronica began to take Nicole more seriously and feared that there would be more to Erika's story. When Erika's trial began, the prosecution team brought up evidence about the murder in Muir Woods, just like Nicole said they would. The prosecution found that Bryan Holmes was beaten to death and left to die. Nicole was not expecting that they would bring two witnesses from Muir Woods to testify on the stand, Erika's ex Tessa Brown, and Jerry Reed.

Erika suddenly became frozen in time. Seeing their faces reminded her of what she tried so hard to forget. Erika always believed that she was set up, and the reason no one ever came looking for her since the murder of Bryan Holmes, was because they would have to admit that they were accomplices in her rape. But seeing Tessa and Jerry testify against her meant that she no longer had any leverage over them. That because the jury and everyone else saw her as a murderer; no one would feel sorry about a rape that happened years ago, especially one she never reported. After hearing their testimonies, Erika took it upon herself to take the stand and speak in her own defense.

"Your honor, I'd like to take the stand," Erika shouted out as she stood up. Nicole was stunned when she heard Erika utter those words, and whispered,

"What the hell are you doing? Sit down and shut up."

The judge agreed for Erika to take the stand, and before she did, Nicole grabbed Erika by the arm and whispered,

"If you go up there and speak, there won't be anything else that I can do for you."

"I'm a murderer; there was never anything you could have done for me."

Erika smiled, leaving Nicole baffled and disappointed. Erika then approached the stand and took a seat.

"Do you swear to tell the truth, the whole truth, and nothing but the truth, so help you, God?"

"I do."

Nicole shook her head in disapproval, and the prosecution began to question her.

"I just have one question for you, the question that everyone here is dying to know. Did you knowingly and with full intent murder Evangeline Williams on the evening of September 25 of this year, and did you also knowingly with full intent murder Bryan Holmes at Muir Woods 10 years ago?"

"Before I answer yes or no, may I have permission to speak freely?" Erika said as she turned to the judge for approval, and he agreed. Erika then glanced over at her friends who were just as baffled as Nicole was. Erika then began to speak.

"The world, this system that you all swear by, is completely backwards. I understand that we are all here for the alleged murders I committed, but has anyone asked what happened to me? My ex-girlfriend and her boyfriend showed up to testify against me today, but they completely left out the part where I was raped, and were fully aware of it, but did nothing to stop it. That's why they never came forward until now; I'm guessing because they felt guilty?"

"Objection!" The prosecution yelled out. Erika glanced over at the judge for permission to continue speaking.

"If I'm going to be sentenced to my death, can

I at least speak?" The judge permitted Erika to continue.

"All my life, people have done nothing but take from me until I literally had nothin else left to give. My soul has been murdered twice over by unkindness, hatred, abuse, and rape. But most of those people who inflicted that pain continue their lives spreading poison to the next person and the next without even a tiny bit of consequence. And ya'll think that mental illness is a disease created in the brain?" Erika chuckled to herself, and proceeded,

"Years ago, I thought I was going on a camping trip with my girlfriend, but it turned out, she wasn't my girlfriend after all. She wasn't even a friend. I was raped, left out in the middle of woods bleeding from my vagina, face shoved into the dirt while bugs crawled inside my mouth, up my thighs. I might physically be alive, but I promise you, I died that night. What would have happened to Bryan if I turned him in? Would he have gotten life in prison for taking away, no stealing my innocence, and my life? You all know the answer to that question.

"Why is my life so undervalued, and someone like Bryan Holmes gets to be mourned? To answer your question, yes! I waited until morning, and at first I thought to run to my car, like I was ordered to. But something inside of me said no, an eye for an eye, a soul for a soul. So I gave that bastard exactly what he deserved. Evangeline too!"

Erika stunned the jury and everyone else, as the room grew quiet. Nicole became emotional after hearing Erika speak; Jasmine and Veronica were emotional as well. They were confused, wondering why they never knew these crucial details about Erika's life. Wondering how it's possible to be friends with a complete stranger. Erika then turned to the judge and said,

"Also, I'd like to change my plea to guilty."

Erika decided that morning that she would admit to her crimes, and made peace with her decision the night before. Nicole knew that there wasn't anything she could do for her friend and that Erika would be spending her life in prison. As the trial came to an end, Erika was found guilty for the charges brought against her. A few days later, Erika was sentenced to life in prison. Erika motioned goodbye to her friends as she nodded her head and smiled. That would be the last time they'd see Erika again. The women left court that day feeling as if they had failed Erika. Though they each felt a certain responsibility to her, they more so felt inspired to take a more in-depth look into their own lives and the choices they've made.

A few days since the trial ended, Nicole had time to do some inner soul searching. Nicole made plans with Robyn, and they were to meet at one of their favorite local Indian restaurants for dinner. Robyn arrived wearing a long olive green dress; her beauty once again amazed Nicole. They both sat down and were served glasses of water while they placed their orders.

"Thank you for inviting me to dinner; I haven't been back here in years," Robyn said.

"Yeah, me too! I remember we would come here every weekend, or when there was something to celebrate," Nicole smiled.

"I'm sorry about your friend; I know that it hasn't been easy for you."

"I'm fine; I'm more concerned about Erika. Hearing what she's been through, it hurts knowing that she felt she couldn't confide in anyone, that we were friends all these years, and there was a lot I didn't know about her."

"Have you spoken to her since?" Robyn asked after taking a sip of water.

"No, and I feel bad, I've been sort of avoiding the whole situation, though I do plan to visit her this weekend. But I didn't ask you here to talk about Erika. I'd like to talk about us."

"Oh, is there a, us now?" Robyn smiled as she became hopeful for the two of them to rebuild their relationship. However, Nicole had other plans.

"That's what I need to talk to you about. Since this whole thing happened with Erika, I had a lot of time to think, and I decided I'm going to stay with my husband. My family needs me."

"Right...of course, they do," Robyn replied with sarcasm as she slammed her cup down.

"I don't want to hurt you." Nicole reached for Robyn's hand, and she turned her away.

"Then why did you call me the other day at three in the morning begging me to...you know what, if you want to spend the rest of your life living in denial, then keep me out of it."

"Denial? I'm not living in denial. I'm doing what I should have done. I chose to be with Daniel, and now I have to live with him. I can't just run off into the sunset with you, no matter how much my heart wants to, no matter how badly I want to be with you, I have to do what's right."

"I can't do this. You think that committing yourself to someone you don't even love, is the right thing to do?" Robyn folded her arms in frustration.

"If I didn't have the kids…"

"You'd still be with him because you don't have the guts to tell him the truth. You are fucking gay! When the hell are you going to stop hiding behind your kids?" Nicole became silent, as she sat back in her seat, and Robyn continued to speak,

"This is the last time I will let you play this merry go round game with me. If this is the choice you're going to make, you better be damn sure it's the right one. Because if it is Daniel, I swear you will never see me again, ever!"

Robyn got up from the table, leaving Nicole with one difficult choice to make.

Later on that evening, Jasmine was getting ready for bed. She had been sleeping on Nicole's couch for almost a week now. Jasmine wasn't sure what her next move would be, but she knew that she couldn't go back to the place she once called home. Nicole, Daniel, and the kids were already upstairs getting ready for bed. Jasmine stretched her legs on the couch, with a book on her lap and a cup of coffee in her hand.

Then suddenly, she heard a loud banging coming from the front door. That startled Jasmine, causing her to spill a little bit of coffee on herself. Nicole and Daniel rushed downstairs, confused about who would be banging on their door at nine o'clock at night. Jasmine watched from the couch as she slowly removed the covers and sat up. Nicole answered the door,

"Why the hell are you banging on my door like a psycho?" Nicole was surprised and deeply disturbed when she noticed Bobby standing on the other side.

"I need to talk to my wife." Bobby then pushed his way inside, knocking Nicole out of the way, but Bobby didn't realize that Daniel was standing next to Nicole, and he quickly became baffled.

"Look, I'm sorry, man, I need to talk to my wife. I'm sure you'd understand." Bobby noticed Jasmine sitting on the couch and approached,

"Get up, you need to come home," Bobby said sternly.

"I don't know what the hell is wrong with you; that place was never my home. And you're stupid if you think I'm going anywhere with you after what you did."

Daniel approached and noticed the tension between the two of them brewing.

"Listen, you can't just barge your way into our home, disrespecting my wife, I need you to leave."

"I didn't disrespect anyone," Bobby replied. He was outnumbered because not a single person wanted him in that home, but he continued to speak to Jasmine.

"Alright, that's how you want to play it, you'll be back, like all the other times. I'll just wait for you to get your shit. If it's even still there by then."

Bobby threatened Jasmine and quickly brushed past Daniel and Nicole leaving the house. Daniel and Nicole were concerned for Jasmine and wanted to make sure she was okay. Jasmine, on the other hand, felt embarrassed about the situation.

"He's right; I should leave. I don't want to cause any problems for you guys."

"You are not causing any problems. I just hope that you really are done with that man for good. He's never going to stop, but you can!"

Nicole was hopeful that Jasmine would be done with Bobby this time. Nicole encouraged Jasmine to focus on her own life, although she knew how hard it would be for Jasmine to leave Bobby. Nicole understood the fear of having to start life over, rebuilding, and rebuilding alone.

The next morning, Erika was continuing to adjust to her new life in prison as she woke in her cell. It's been a week since Erika was sentenced, and has yet to receive a visit from her friends. Nicole and Jasmine both reached out by phone, but still not a word from Veronica. Erika woke up this particular morning in tears, and for the first time, she felt completely alone. Erika began to believe that she would die in prison, alone. This thought bothered Erika, it tormented her, and she began to have chest pains from all the tears she cried.

Erika then had the idea to reach out by writing her friends a letter. Erika had the cell to herself, which allowed her to have a tiny bit of peace under the circumstances. Erika reached under the mattress for her hidden pen and notebook. Erika was the kind of person who kept journals and diaries; it helped her to sort through her emotions. As Erika began to write, her thoughts carried away,

I'm not even sure where to begin; I guess I can begin with Thank You. Thank you for being my friends, even though I have disappointed you, abused your trust, and didn't appreciate the love you all gave me to the fullest. Don't think that you each weren't valued, or that I didn't love and appreciate you because I did, truly. I wish I could take back the things that I've done, but I can't. I wish that I could be normal, but I'm not. I wish that my heart wasn't so broken, but it is.

Erika continued writing as she explained her feelings, hopes, and wishes for her friends. Erika mostly apologized to Veronica and admitted that her sleeping with Gloria was in fact, a lie. Erika wanted to give Veronica that peace of mind so that she could move forward with her life.

I would never do that to you, Veronica. The crazy thing is, I was jealous and didn't understand why you never chose me. I felt more alone in the world when you met Gloria. I wanted to keep you all to myself, but instead, I lost you completely, and for that, I'm sorry.

Erika knew that she made a wrong turn at some point in her life, one that she couldn't come back from. Erika believed in the moment as she was writing that her soul wasn't redeemable. The only thing she could think to do was to offer her friends some wisdom.

I hope that you guys can learn from me. Stop living life pretending to be someone you're not, only to satisfy a world that doesn't give a shit about you. Don't settle into a marriage that's literally on the verge of killing you, just because you're afraid to get out and start over. Trust me, starting over will be the only thing to set you free. But most importantly, forgive; don't hold on to the pain, it's a growing decay that rots away at your soul, hinders you from seeing the light in the world. You are strong, beautiful women, and I just want you to be happy, be free, and, most importantly, be you. I love you now and forever. See you all on the brighter side.

Erika shed a tear as she finished her letter, and began folding it into threes. Erika felt a sense of relief as she freed herself from her last lie. She then glanced around the room, inhaled, and exhaled slowly. Erika then waited until it was mealtime to have her letter mailed. She sat alone, enjoyed her morning breakfast, which consisted of cold eggs, and a slice of toast. At this point, Erika knew there was no need to complain, but to simply take each moment, and appreciate the good that came with it.

After meal period, Erika decided to take a shower. Of course, she wanted to smell fresh in the morning, so she gathered all of her things, and carefully headed down the hall past the guards. Once inside the shower room, Erika found a stall, took off her clothes, and placed them over the wall beside her. Finally, Erika turned on the shower, feeling the warm water vibrate against her skin. She inhaled and exhaled once more as her body began to relax. Erika then began to trace the water with an object as it dripped onto her arm, drawing a large flower. She started with the stem and made her way down to her wrists, outlining a rosebud. Erika continued the same movement on her other arm. But before she could finish, she became lightheaded and slowly fell to the ground, with her back against the shower wall. The water continued to spray over her body, and from her body to the ground formed a red puddle. Erika looked up at the light and said,

"Please, God, reunite me with love."

As quickly as Erika said those words, her eye closed. The puddle grew larger, spreading over to the next shower stall, alerting a couple of the other inmates. They rushed over and were shaken by what they saw. Erika died that morning.

Her friends, Nicole, Jasmine, and Veronica, had no idea of what happened. They were too busy dealing with their own problems. It wasn't until a couple of days later when Nicole received a letter in the mail that she knew, or had a hint that something may have happened to Erika. Nicole rushed to the prison, hoping her thoughts were wrong, and she called Jasmine and Veronica on the way.

"Did you guys receive a letter in the mail from Erika?"

"No, why," Veronica replied with little concern.

"I think she may have committed suicide."

"What, no way, why would you say that?" Jasmine asked.

"Because of what she wrote in this letter, the way that she worded certain things sounds to me like a suicide note. Have you guys tried to call or visit her?"

"Honestly, I don't have any plans of visiting or calling her. I'm done with Erika, and you guys should be two."

"You need to read the letter Veronica, you both do," Nicole said sternly.

Nicole hung up the phone and continued making her way to the prison. When Nicole arrived, she was shocked when she found out that Erika had committed suicide two days ago. Nicole was disgusted with herself, upset that she didn't even know her good friend was deceased. More importantly, Nicole felt a massive regret for not visiting Erika; she said to herself, *maybe if Erika knew that she was loved, she would have stayed alive.* Both Jasmine and Veronica finally read the letter that Nicole received. On the day of Erika's funeral, which Nicole paid for, she, Jasmine, and surprisingly Veronica were the only three who attended. They each watched as her casket was laid into the ground, and Nicole had a few words for the women.

"This was our fault."

"Our?" Veronica said with confusion.

"Yes, our! We neglected her when she needed us most. Damn it; we fucking let her die in prison, alone. Not one of us even went by to visit," Nicole cried out.

"But you know why I didn't visit, why I couldn't, it was too much. I didn't think that I could forgive her," Veronica said.

"Yeah, well, whether you forgive her or not, she's still dead because we failed her. We failed her as friends. But I will honor her memory, her death. I'm going to starting living my life; I'm going to be me!" Nicole said as she stared into the ground at Erika's casket.

"Then, I guess I should honor her memory too, and finally free myself from my fuckin marriage." Jasmine said, and then turned to Veronica to say,

"What are you going to do?"

"I'm going to try to forgive her. I mean she's gone, what's hating her now going to do for me?"

Later that day, each of the women made choices, choices that were inspired by Erika's life, and death. Nicole decided to finally have that long-awaited talk with Daniel she'd been avoiding for years. Nicole laid everything out on the table, even knowing the consequences she may reap from her honesty. Nicole sat Daniel down at the foot of their bed and began speaking about the affairs.

"Daniel, I'm so sorry that I wasn't honest with you before."

"How long, how long have you been having these affairs?"

"Does that matter?" Nicole asked while Daniel stared grimly.

"For about six or seven years."

"Damn it, Nicole! I was faithful to you! I can't believe I was this stupid." Daniel quickly hopped off the bed and began pacing the room.

"I'm truly sorry, Daniel. I tried to tell you multiple times who I am, but you refused to believe me."

"So, this is my fault. I'm the reason you started whoring around town?" Nicole became insulted and quickly got up and approached Daniel.

"Don't you dare, don't you dare call me that. I told you that I wanted to see other people. I told you that I believed I was gay, and you never took me seriously. I felt like I had to force my true feelings away and shove them in the damn closet to protect you and make you happy. That's not living; it's just fucking existing."

"So, what are you saying? Is this something you can stop, are you going to fucking stop having these gay feelings?"

"You're not listening again! What do I have to say to get you to hear me? Daniel, I'm in love with someone else."

At that moment, Daniel froze, and for the first time, he couldn't pretend or deny the truth that Nicole was screaming out.

"How could you do this to me, to us? We have a family, did you even think about that at all?"

"Of course, I did! Why do you think I tried so hard to push my feelings away, to push myself away? Daniel, you and the kids are my world. You are my best friend. I didn't want to lose that. But the feelings you have for me, that I should have for you to make this marriage work, I just don't have."

"Then figure out a damn way to have them!" Nicole became frustrated as she could tell she wasn't getting through to Daniel.

"Daniel, I'm going to move out, that's the only way you will take me at least half-seriously."

Daniel was heartbroken, as he knew he didn't have any choice but to hear her. Daniel wanted revenge; he wanted to make things as difficult for her as possible. Of course, he tried to take full custody of the children, but with Nicole being a lawyer, he realized it would be better to have her as a friend and not as an enemy. In the end, Daniel held on to their friendship and put on a brave face for the kids. After all, they were friends first before anything. And although his heart was broken, he didn't want to force Nicole to be with him any longer. Daniel and Nicole filed for divorce a week later. Nicole was finally free, free to be whoever she wanted to be.

Veronica, however, was still dealing with the grief of losing her best friend, Erika. Although she spent most of the time hating Erika, there was still a large part of Veronica that loved her. Since Erika's betrayal, Veronica put up walls of protection, but she didn't realize that she put those walls up against Gloria as well. This particular morning, it was a Sunday, Veronica was sleeping in, and Gloria decided to make her a surprise breakfast in bed.

"Good morning, my love." Gloria walked into the room, waking Veronica up with the smell of crispy bacon, eggs mixed with spinach and mushroom. She also had a glass of orange juice. Gloria sat the tray down over Veronica's lap and watched as she smiled from ear to ear.

"Honey, you did all this for me?"

"Si, I hope you enjoy."

"What about you? Comer?"

"No, I'm fine." Gloria said, "Pero, I'll have some

orange juice." Gloria smiled as she took a sip of Veronica's orange juice. Veronica hadn't noticed yet that Gloria's English seemed to have improved as she was communicating and understanding her better. Veronica took a bite of her crispy bacon and indulged while also offering Gloria a taste. The two continued to sit on the bed, and Gloria became nervous.

"Are you okay?" Veronica said with a mouth full of bacon.

"Yes, there's something I need to say."

Gloria began to speak to Veronica, very fluently in fact, which stunned and surprised her. Gloria was working up the courage to propose to Veronica. Though they are already married, their first wedding was at the courthouse. Gloria always wanted to have a do-over, a celebration where their families and friends could join. Gloria continued to speak fluently to Veronica, but Veronica interrupted in amazement.

"Wait a minute, are you speaking in fluent English right now? Were you able to speak clear English this whole time?"

"No," Gloria laughed to herself. "No, that's what I'm trying to tell you, please can I finish?"

Veronica nodded her head, yes, and Gloria then took Veronica's hand and gently placed it in hers.

"I love you! I love you so much, you don't realize how happy you have made me, even when you're ranting away and shouting, I love you. We had some rough times, but we always got through them together. I didn't know what Erika was doing that night years ago; I didn't know what she was planning or why. But since then, I took it upon myself to study the English language so that I wouldn't be left in the dark again.

"I swear that I would never hurt you like that, no matter how bad things may get. I felt like you needed to hear that, in English." Gloria smiled, and Veronica sat there with her eyes wide as an owl, still amazed hearing Gloria speak to her in fluent English. Gloria then reached into the nightstand and pulled out a small box.

"I know this isn't the most romantic place to do this, but Veronica Marie Rodriguez, will you marry me again?" Gloria sat there with the ring box in her hand, and from it shined a beautiful diamond, one that Veronica could not take her eyes off of.

"Oh my God, now I feel so bad, I don't deserve

this. You studied English, learned to communicate with me better, and I didn't even pick up a damn book, or download an app. I don't deserve you."

"Yes you do, we are already married anyway." Gloria laughed, "Just let me do this, I'd like us to have a real wedding, with family and friends. Please, Veronica, will you marry me again?"

"Damn, I can't say no to this ring, or you. I love you! Yes, I will marry you again."

Gloria and Veronica embraced one another, and at that moment, Veronica realized that she didn't need to keep her walls up any longer; Veronica chose to be happy instead. Knowing how much Gloria valued her, hearing how much she loved her was exactly what Veronica needed.

"Can you teach me your language? I'm going to put in the work, and give you 150 percent, just like you've given me. I want to learn as much about your world as I can, and I'm so sorry that I didn't try harder sooner."

"Where do you want to start?"

While Veronica and Gloria were opening a new chapter in their lives, the next day, Jasmine was closing one of her own. Jasmine finally went back to her home after weeks of being away, and to her surprise, Bobby was there waiting. Jasmine hoped she could be in and out, grab the things she needed, but Bobby had other plans. As soon as Jasmine walked through the front door, she could see Bobby to her left sitting in the living room on the couch. Jasmine paused as they both made eye contact, then she quickly headed up the stairs to get her things. Of course, Bobby chased after her and cornered her once they were in the bedroom.

"Jasmine, I'm glad you came back, can we just talk for a minute?"

"I'm not here to talk, I'm here to get the rest of my things."

Jasmine brushed past Bobby and walked into the closet, but he stopped her by grabbing her by the arm.

"Please, just hear me out!" Jasmine yanked her arm out of Bobby's hand.

"Do not put your hands on me! And before you even think about putting your hands around my neck again, I'll ask that nice officer standing outside to come in here and show you what a real man is."

Bobby quickly walked over to the window to call Jasmine's bluff but was surprised when he saw an officer standing outside, leaning against a police car, staring right back at him.

"So you're getting the people at our work involved in our business now?" Bobby walked back over toward Jasmine.

"I'm doing what I should have done a long time ago. You and I, we were never supposed to be together this long. You were a test for me, and I failed year after year after year, but I'm passing the test today, and getting the fuck out of this marriage." Bobby began to plead for Jasmine to stay as he used a softer tone.

"Jasmine, please, I'll do whatever you need me to do, I'll get help."

"You need to get help for yourself, Bobby, not for me. We both do."

Jasmine continued packing her things, and Bobby slowly sat down on the bed.

"Did you ever really love me?" Bobby asked.

"Is love desperate? Is love a replacement for loneliness? Is love when you have to lose yourself because it's better than being alone? Is love...abusive? Bobby, I don't think either of us loved each other. I think we just desperately needed each other to fill a void that can't be filled. I don't want to need someone for the wrong reasons; I want to want them for all the right ones. We have to let each other go so that we can finally find ourselves. Because this, this is not who I want to be."

Jasmine continued packing as Bobby sat on the bed, feeling hopeless and defeated. Deep down, Bobby knew that Jasmine was right, and he began to realize that he couldn't run from himself forever, that he needed to face his demons. Bobby decided at that moment to finally go to counseling. Secretly, Bobby feared what he would learn about himself. He feared being incurable. On this day, Bobby realized he's the only one standing in the way of his happiness.

Bobby and Jasmine filed for a divorce shortly after, but they continued to stay in contact by phone, it was their way of slowly letting each other go. Bobby decided it would be best if he transferred precincts, allowing Jasmine to shine and get promoted to lead detective. Everyone around could see the light finally shining through Jasmine, now that she was out of her abusive marriage. Jasmine also decided to take time for herself before dating anyone new. Although guys and a few women have tried, Jasmine wouldn't be doing any dating anytime soon.

A few months passed since Erika's funeral. Jasmine, Nicole, and Veronica each went to visit Erika's grave. The three of them showed up with flowers, and Jasmine showed up with a pack of Oreo cookies and a small liter of milk. Nicole and Veronica were confused when they noticed Jasmine holing the food in her hand.

"Did you just bring a case of Oreos and some milk? Do you think this is some kind of tea party?" Veronica asked as she laughed from confusion.

"No, Oreos were Erika's favorite. Back when we were in college, we used to share these and a glass of milk, it's my way of being sentimental, jeez!"

"Whatever you say," Veronica continued to laugh.

"I can't believe we are here, standing at Erika's tombstone. I never thought I'd have to bury a friend," Nicole said.

"I know, me either," Jasmine said as she stooped down to place an Oreo on the ground in front of the tombstone. She then proceeded by pouring milk on top, and Veronica continued to stare.

"This is supposed to be a sad day, and you keep making me laugh with that shit."

"Would you like one?" Jasmine asked, and Veronica took a moment to think about it.

"Damn it, give it here." Jasmine gave Veronica a cookie, took one out for Nicole, and then herself. They each sat down in front of Erika's tombstone, sharing Oreos while remembering Erika's life.

"Do you think she's in heaven?" Veronica asked.

"I don't know, I don't think heaven is a place, but a feeling. I just hope that wherever she is, she's loved, happy, and free." Nicole said as she took another bite of her Oreo.

"Well, Bobby and I are getting a divorce."

"About damn time, I would drink to that if I had some alcohol." Nicole said, and the women chuckled.

"Well Gloria and I, we're getting married in a couple of months."

"Wait, I thought you guys were already married?" Jasmine said with confusion.

"We are but, we're going to have an actual ceremony, and she got me this," Veronica showed off her new shiny rock.

"Damn! I didn't know Gloria had it like that

being an artist; maybe I need to change careers." Nicole said jokingly while she admired Veronica's ring.

"I'm happy for you, I am, and I bet Erika is too."

"Thanks, I hope she is. So what about you and Daniel, how are you guys?"

"We've filed for a divorce actually. Daniel and I are still friends, but I've moved out, and I decided to follow my heart."

"Wait. What! Why didn't you call me? You need to fill me all the way in." Jasmine replied.

"Ah, yeah, me too"! Veronica said as she sat closer.

"Well, Robyn and I, we're taking things slow, but I've never been happier. I can finally exhale and smile."

"That's really good, Nicole, I'm happy for you. I mean, I do feel bad for Daniel." Jasmine interrupted.

"I did too, but I think he's going to be okay, especially since he seemed to have quickly moved on with that damn teacher."

"What teacher?" Jasmine asked.

"Ms. Brown"! Nicole sighed.

Nicole filled the women in on Daniel and his

new love interest. They each sat there by Erika's grave for the rest of the evening talking and sharing stories. These women seemed to have learned a lot about themselves and each other over the past year. They learned to move together more like sisters and to not take moments for granted, or one another. The biggest lesson these women seemed to have learned was just how short life really is, and what you do with it matters. It affects not only you but also those around you. They could continue their cycled programed living by staying in a abusive relationship, hiding from the truth, holding on to pain and grudges, or prevail, forgive, and being free.

A couple of months later, Jasmine was all moved of her old home with Bobby, and into a new flat in downtown San Francisco. The sun was shining just right; the weather was a chilly 76, and she decided to get out for a morning jog. Jasmine proudly jogged down the busy streets as she listened to her tunes dressed in her new Nike sports attire. As Jasmine inhaled and exhaled the beautiful view ahead, mountains and the ocean from afar, she ran into a familiar face.

"Oh my God, sorry, how are you." Jasmine said as she tried to catch her breath.

"I'm doing well. I decided to take your advice; I've been seeing a therapist a couple of times a week, you seem well." Bobby replied with a smile.

"Yeah, I am. But I'm really happy for you." Jasmine smiled back while jogging in place, and Bobby stared back in awe.

"Well, I gotta go."

"Wait, Jasmine!" Bobby stopped Jasmine from jogging away as she stood and listened.

"I just want to say, I'm sorry for everything that I've put you through. I'm sorry that I abused you not only physically but also mentally. I wish I spent that time getting to know you. You'll always be the one who got away. I know I don't even deserve to have you standing here, listening to me right now, but I hope that one day, maybe we can be friends?"

"I don't know, maybe when we are both too old to fight, who knows. I need you to understand, I can never allow myself to go there again. But, I do wish you well, and I hope that you continue to take care of yourself, Bobby, and thank you...for the sincerity."

Bobby smiled as he watched Jasmine jog away, but kept a slither of hope that one day, he could earn his way back into her heart. Jasmine, however, was inhaling and exhaling freedom, as she knew she was leaving Bobby in the distance of her mind. Jasmine felt proud knowing she took back her power, and that no one else would ever have control over her life again. Jasmine heeded Erika's last words, *be happy, be free, be you.* And that's precisely what she and her friends will be!

www.ingramcontent.com/pod-product-compliance
Lightning Source LLC
Chambersburg PA
CBHW021404290426
44108CB00010B/382